Fit for the Leadership Challenge

The key to effective leadership is being fit for the challenge. Leadership is a perpetual boxing match in many respects in which preparation, stamina and skill are required. Only the strongest survive. Every decision and tollgate along the career journey is laden with risk. Those leaders who harness risk to their advantage will land the knockout punch in every fight. The only question is how many leaders will be fit enough for the challenge?

The purpose of this book is to provide insight as to how risk impacts every aspect of leadership, including the mundane, routine and nonglamorous aspects of leadership. This is important because often the small things can easily turn into big disruptors. Moreover, the end goal is to equip leaders with a journey map and quick guide to win in high-risk environments. Change is the new normal and only constant in today's world. As change increases, so will risk and its subsequent impacts on humanity. This includes leaders, organizations and customers. No one is exempt.

In this book, readers learn how to:

- Determine which career battles to fight and which ones to avoid.
- Prepare to fight the unavoidable challenges along the career journey.
- Leverage risk to choose the right leaders for the team.
- Leverage risk to invest time wisely and avoid wasting it.
- Leverage risk to predict, identify and resolve leadership burnout.
- Risk assess leadership credentials so only those that produce a return are added to the portfolio.
- Risk assess performance outcomes so the path ahead is smooth sailing instead of a rough ride.
- Leverage risk so high performance is a reality instead of a pipe dream.
- Leverage risk to find the right leadership sponsor.

Fit for the Leadership Challenge

The 17 Keys Leaders Need to Win
Big in High-Risk Environments

Casey J. Bedgood

Routledge
Taylor & Francis Group

A PRODUCTIVITY PRESS BOOK

First published 2023
by Routledge
605 Third Avenue, New York, NY 10158

and by Routledge
4 Park Square, Milton Park, Abingdon, Oxon, OX14 4RN

Routledge is an imprint of the Taylor & Francis Group, an informa business

ISBN: 978-1-032-37058-3 (hbk)
ISBN: 978-1-032-37056-9 (pbk)
ISBN: 978-1-003-33510-8 (ebk)

DOI: 10.4324/9781003335108

Typeset in Garamond
by Apex CoVantage, LLC

Contents

About the Author

Casey J. Bedgood is an author, thought leader and master change agent with over 20 years of healthcare leadership experience. He is the author of *The Ride of a Lifetime*, *The Ideal Performance Improvement Eco System*, *The ABCs of Designing Performance Improvement Programs*, *Conquering the Giants*, *Fit for the Leadership Challenge*, *The Mystery of Leadership* and *The Power of Organizational Knowledge*. He is a Six Sigma Black Belt and accomplished author. Over the years, Bedgood's work has been recognized, sourced and modeled by national and global best practice organizations in the healthcare industry and beyond. He has amassed a portfolio of dozens of publications on topics such as thought leadership, knowledge transfer, performance improvement, strategic design, innovative thinking, transformation, Quality Management System (QMS) and many others. Subsequently, many large, complex healthcare enterprises across the US, Canada and Singapore have sourced and sought after Bedgood's thought leadership expertise.

Bedgood earned a bachelor of business administration, magna cum laude, from Mercer University and a master of public administration from Georgia College and State University. He is an IISE Lean Green Belt, Six Sigma Green Belt and Six Sigma Black Belt. Also, he is Change Acceleration Process trained via GE and a member of the American College of Healthcare Executives.

Introduction

Are leaders all knowing? Is measurement of the current-state risk a leadership requirement or can leaders simply wing it? Do leaders really understand risk and its impact on their career, organization and customer base? Is ignorance always bliss or a catalyst for disruption? Does risk apply to unconventional aspects of leadership such as selecting next-level roles, promoting subordinates, the leadership brand, variation, burnout, performance outcomes and the like? Is it possible to leverage risk assessment tools to predict future performance, missteps and potential potholes along the leadership journey? Can proper risk assessments guide leaders along their career journey to ensure they always find the oasis and avoid the mirage? We discuss these and other topics in the sections that follow.

The purpose of this book is to provide insight as to how risk impacts every aspect of leadership, including the mundane, routine and nonglamorous aspects of leadership. This is important because often the small things can easily turn into big disruptors. Moreover, the end goal is to equip leaders, aspiring leaders, students and anyone interested in leadership with a journey map and quick guide to win in high-risk environments. Change is the new normal and only constant in today's world. As change increases, so will risk and its subsequent impacts on humanity. This includes leaders, organizations and customers. No one is exempt.

The genesis of the book stems from a conversation between a top leader in the service industry and a young up-and-coming thought leader. One day, the thought leader arrived in C-Suite for a meeting with several top leaders. Out of the blue, the organization's CEO stepped out of an office and walked up to the young thought leader with a big smile.

DOI: 10.4324/9781003335108-1

The CEO gracefully grabbed the thought leader by the arm and said, 'Young man, put on your boxing gloves.' The thought leader was taken aback by the comments and had no reference for its meaning. Several senior leaders standing in the office suite began to laugh at the comments. It was like everyone was in on the joke except this young, high-flying leader.

The reality was that the thought leader soon was put on a fast track to assume senior leadership roles and responsibilities. The adage of 'crocodile-infested waters' applied unknowingly. The CEO was offering a pearl of wisdom before the rocket ship took off. The senior leaders laughed because they understood the implication and knew the trials, tests, challenges and potholes this young, naive leader was about to face.

For generations, leaders have been schooled in formal academic programs. Young leaders and those aspiring are let out of the gate (professionally speaking) with various degrees, credentials and the like. They seem so confident that they are ready to tackle the world's problems as leaders. In reality, they are ill prepared and naïve, and the career path that appears to be sparkling is laden with land mines. As it has been said, 'everything that sparkles does not always shine.' The key is that perception is not always reality.

As the young thought leader progressed, the years ahead were full of accolades, historical milestones and impossibilities that became possible. But, it didn't come easy. Risk was ever present. Often, leaders simply didn't know what they didn't measure. The leader realized early on that everything has a risk. Risk applies to the mundane aspects of leadership we often overlook. The adage of 'if it was a snake, it would have bitten you' was the recurring theme along the journey.

The young leader learned quickly that leadership is a risky business. Along the journey, leaders who can identify, measure, analyze and mitigate risks will have the greatest chance of survival. The key is being fit for the fight. Leadership is a perpetual boxing match in many respects in which preparation, stamina and skill are required. Only the strongest survive.

Leaders will have to wrestle with decisions about taking or passing on next-level roles, who to promote, participating in activities that can enhance or destroy their brand, sharing information or holding it close to the vest, addressing variation and inconsistent performance outcomes, preventing and identifying burnout for themselves and others, investing in credentials or using time more wisely and so many other attributes of leadership. The key is that each decision and tollgate along the career journey is laden with risk. Those leaders who harness risk to their advantage will land the knockout punch in every fight. The only question is how many leaders will be fit enough for the fight?

In the following chapters, readers will gain great insight into practical applications of risk that most leaders never realize are present or impactful. Moreover, *Fit for the Leadership Challenge: The 17 Keys Leaders Need to Win Big in High-Risk Environments* will lay out a guide to help leaders and those aspiring to find sure footing with each step instead of a series of perpetual career potholes.

Chapter 1

Leveraging Risk to Determine Organizational Efficiency: Is High Performance a Reality or a Pipe Dream?

Why Efficiency Matters

Efficiency can be defined as, 'A situation in which a person, company, factory, etc. uses resources such as time, materials, or labor well, without wasting any' (1). In layman's terms, efficiency is simply using the least amount of resources to accomplish a task. It's common for thought leaders to consider efficiency synonymous with high performance. High performance can have different meanings based on the industry and area of focus. But, the premise is that it's good for organizations to do more with less, eliminate waste and perform at higher levels. The end goal is to maximize the value each customer receives when touching the organization at any point.

There are several considerations worth noting when considering this concept. Why does efficiency matter? Is efficiency important to leaders regardless of industry? Are all organizations efficient? Is efficiency an inherent attribute in operations, or does it require intentional actions to function better? Is efficiency associated with risk? Can high levels of risk prevent organizations from achieving higher levels of performance? Is efficiency

DOI: 10.4324/9781003335108-2

multifactorial or simply achieved with minimal effort? Can leaders use a simple risk tool to assess and predict their organization's potential of being efficient? We answer these and more considerations in the sections that follow.

Levels of Efficiency

When striving for higher levels of performance, leaders and their organizations must consider several levels. The levels of efficiency include the individual, a department, an entity or division and the enterprise as a whole. See Figure 1 for details.

Higher performance is predicated on teamwork where all individuals and teams perform better. The higher the level as noted in Figure 1, the greater is the efficiency impact on the organization and its customers. The theme here is that more is better. Thus, high performance is the intended goal.

For example, if one employee interacts with 100 customers per year and reduces customer wait time by 5 minutes per interaction, then the efficiency gained is good. But, it's very minimal. The overall efficiency gained is 500 minutes or roughly 8 hours of waiting.

If all team members in the department perform better and reduce customer wait times by 5 minutes for 10,000 customers, then the gain is much more impactful. The impact is 50,000 minutes saved or the equivalent of 833 hours. Irrespectively, the point is that leaders should strive for global (organizationally speaking) efficiency gains. The end game is to find ways of performing better that impact the greatest amount of people. The higher the organizational level of efficiency, the greater is the impact on humanity, generally speaking.

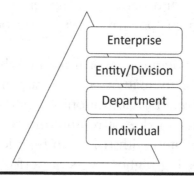

Figure 1   Levels of Efficiency.

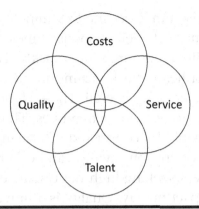

Figure 1.1 Areas of Efficiency.

Target Areas of Efficiency

Another aspect of higher-level performance is the target areas of efficiency efforts. There are four basic targets that leaders should focus on when beginning the journey to higher performance. See Figure 1.1 for details.

First, many organizations and their leaders typically gravitate to financial efficiencies. If we improve 'x,' how much money will we save? The key here is that cost savings can emerge in two forms: hard dollar savings and soft savings.

Hard dollar savings is as straightforward as it sounds. When a leader or team improves, hard dollar savings represent tangible and measurable dollars savings that impact the financial statement. In contrast, soft savings represent improvements in 'something' that may not have direct dollar savings. Let's take a look at a couple examples.

A healthcare organization deploys a Six Sigma Black Belt to help an ambulance service with emergency response time delays. The goal is 10 minutes or less 90% of the time for emergency 911 responses. Think of an ambulance responding to wrecks, gunshots, heart attacks and the like. The ambulance service's current performance is 12 minutes per 911 call on average 80% of the time.

The team conducts an assessment and analyzes the current state. Next, they implement several solutions that include changing the deployment plan where ambulances are stationed strategically in high call volume areas. The result is significant reductions in emergency response times and miles traveled. By traveling fewer miles, the service realizes $100,000 in hard dollar savings related to fleet costs. Fewer miles equates to less fuel wasted, fewer mechanical repairs per ambulance, and so on.

In contrast, the response times decline to 9 minutes per call on average 90% of the time. These more efficient response times ensure critically ill and injured patients receive lifesaving care more quickly. Thus, over the course of the first year, hundreds of heart attack victims are saved, have shorter hospital stays and have better outcomes overall. These clinical efficiencies result in a 30% improvement in customer satisfaction rates. Thus, the improvements or efficiencies in this lens would be considered soft savings. Irrespectively, this example shows how important soft savings can be to humanity.

Second, thought leaders seeking high performance should consider how efficiency efforts will impact quality. Quality is a universal concept regardless of industry. Whether leaders are providing emergency health services or manufacturing electronics used by flyers in the Air Force, the goal is higher quality. The end game is to provide the highest level of quality in goods or services. Moreover, this will only occur with a good, consistent and highly reliable process.

Third, higher-performing organizations should consider impacts of efficiency efforts on service. Service is typically measured by customer satisfaction or customer experience. The key is to ensure leaders know who their customers are and what they want and have created processes that repeatedly meet and exceed customer requirement. In this sense, better service is always ideal.

Fourth, leaders must consider the organization's talent in the journey for higher-level performance. The reality is that organizations are made up of people. People determine the organization's culture. Also, culture determines how work is done. If culture is aligned properly, then efficiency can be a very real possibility. If culture is not aligned, higher-level performance will quickly become a pipe dream.

The key is to ensure culture is aligned with the organization's mission, vision, values, norms and overall trajectory. Often, culture is the deciding factor as to if the enterprise will improve or stagnate. The takeaway is that people matter, and they determine if the organization will realize efficiencies in costs, quality and service. Let's take a look at how one organization used a simple risk tool to determine its efficiency potential.

Case Study

Recently, a top leader of a very large service company held a press conference. The leader outlined the organization's growth strategy via several multibillion-dollar acquisitions of competitors in several markets in one state.

The announcements sent a shockwave through the industry. The term 'Pac-Man' immediately came to mind.

The top leader espoused that their organization was the market leader in this industry based on four factors: low costs, high quality, the best service and efficiency. Did you miss the last attribute? Yes, the leader's flag at the top of the industry's flagpole was predicated on efficiency or high performance. In layman's terms, the leader simply told its customer base and competitors that their organization could provide services better, faster and cheaper than anyone else. Also, the outcomes of the enterprise were higher quality and higher customer satisfaction than any rivals.

After the announcement, leaders in other organizations assembled teams in their 'war rooms' to ensure their operating postures could withstand this invasion from the competitor. One organization used a simple risk assessment tool as part of the analysis. The internal perception was that the business was strong, well run and ready for the fight with encroaching competitors.

See Figure 1.2 for details.

The team started by listing all the major business units in the organization. Next, the team scored each entity on several attributes, such as operational goal attainment, culture, strategic planning and knowledge transfer. There are two considerations for goal attainment. The team measured how successful the enterprise was in achieving base goals and stretch goals. For example, what percentage of base goals tied to quality were achieved each year? Once the base goals were achieved, how well did the organization pivot and meet quality stretch goals? The operational goals were tied to service, cost and quality of services.

The team also measured the organization's culture in various business units. Was the culture unifocal or multifaceted? Was the culture change acceptant, change resistant or neutral to change? Was the culture aligned with the organization's strategy? Ideally, the organization from top to bottom would be champions of change and forward thinking.

For strategic planning and organizational knowledge, the leaders determined the degree of maturity with both attributes. Did the enterprise have a strategic planning process that occurred each time every year? Was the strategy process hardwired into the culture? Did the planning process include a proper gap analysis, risk assessment, goal setting and execution strategy for all business units?

In terms of knowledge, the leaders considered several factors. The team focused on turnover, as this is a direct impact factor of quality. In some

Business Unit	Organization's Base Goal Attainment 1->90% 2-70%-90% 3-<70%	Organization's Stretch Goal Attainment 1->90% 2-70%-90% 3-<70%	Organizational Culture 1-Change Acceptant 2-Change Neutral 3-Change Resistant	Strategic Planning Process 1- Mature System Process linking gaps-goals-outcomes 2- Silo Process with mixed outcomes in gaps-goals-outcomes 3-No Process with no links in gaps-goals-outcomes	Knowledge Transfer Program? 1- Mature 2- Beginner 3-No Program	Risk Score *Sum Columns 2-6 Lower Score = Lower Risk	Efficiency Potential
Unit 1	3	3	3	3	2	14	Low
Unit 2	3	3	2	3	2	13	Low
Unit 3	2	2	1	2	1	8	High
Unit 4	3	3	3	3	2	14	Low
Unit 5	2	2	1	2	1	8	High

Avg Score	2.7	2.7	2.0	2.7	1.7	
Risk Level	High Risk	High Risk	Low Risk	High Risk	Low Risk	

Max Risk	15
Lowest Risk	5
Avg Risk	10

Figure 1.2   Efficiency Risk Assessment Tool.

instances, when turnover is high, organizational knowledge declines. Thus, quality of services is less than desired. They also focused on succession planning, depth of roles for critical positions and cross training. The key here is more knowledge is better.

Figure 1.2 outlines the results for five business units. Sixty percent of the business units had low potential to be efficient or high performing. In contrast, 40% of the organization was high performing. The higher performers had aligned cultures. Thus, goal attainment tied to operations was higher.

Moreover, these business units scored higher on organizational knowledge and strategic planning. In short, the leaders of these high-performing areas successfully aligned strategy, outcomes, knowledge and risk. The higher the performance or efficiency, the lower is the risk of being disrupted by the competitor. The takeaway was the organization had bright spots and burning issues.

Overall, the majority of the organization was at high risk to be disrupted. Thus, 'Pac-Man' appearing on the enterprise's front doorstep was closer than leaders expected. Was leadership perception the reality in this case? Arguably not.

Summary

The key is that perception is not always reality. What leaders think they know may be reality or simply a pipe dream. The key to succeeding in high-risk markets is insight. Simply put, leaders and their organizations that risk score their performance will be better prepared to address market turbulence such as encroachment from competitors.

Efficiency does matter in many ways. Higher performance will ensure organizations can fend off encroachment from competitors, retain their current customer base, grow the enterprise footprint, maximize revenues, minimize costs and ensure service is impeccable for each customer at every organizational touchpoint. In short, efficiency is the key that unlocks the door to organizational longevity.

In summary, change is the new normal and only constant. Change breeds risk. Risk can be leveraged for higher-level performance if recognized early and harnessed. If risk is not identified and mitigated properly, it can be a great disruptor. The key is that leaders don't know what they don't measure. Ignorance is never bliss. Thus, the adage 'measure twice and cut once' applies.

The key to ensuring organizational efficiency is a true reality instead of a pipe dream is predicated on process. Those leaders who master the art of aligning strategy, knowledge, outcomes and risk will realize the greatest efficiency potential. Unfortunately, those who miss the forest for the trees will be the next case study.

Reference

1. Cambridge Dictionary. Efficiency. https://dictionary.cambridge.org/us/dictionary/english/efficiency

Chapter 2

Is Finding the Right Leadership Sponsor Risky Business?

Sponsorship

Merriam-Webster defines leadership as 'The office or position of a leader.' Practically, leadership is essentially getting others to do what you want without force. Is there an art and science to becoming an effective leader? The short answer is yes.

One of the greatest challenges leaders face along the career journey is minimizing risks. Career risks may include acquiring the right skills, continuing education, aligning with the right career partners, knowing when to step forward for the next role and the like. Unfortunately, formal education does not always properly prepare one to master the art of leadership.

There are several fundamentals leaders must master to be effective in the long term. See Figure 2 for details.

First, leaders and those aspiring must prepare themselves with the minimum knowledge, skills and abilities (KSAs). KSAs are synonymous with base knowledge and typically entry-level credentials. These attributes are typically gained during formal training or academic programs. Again, the great aspect of formal training is that it provides insight into the science of leadership. But, what about the art of leading others?

These skills tend to be learned over time through experience. The adage of 'the school of hard knocks' applies here. Fortunately, some of the best life lessons come through experience. The problem is that not all experience

DOI: 10.4324/9781003335108-3

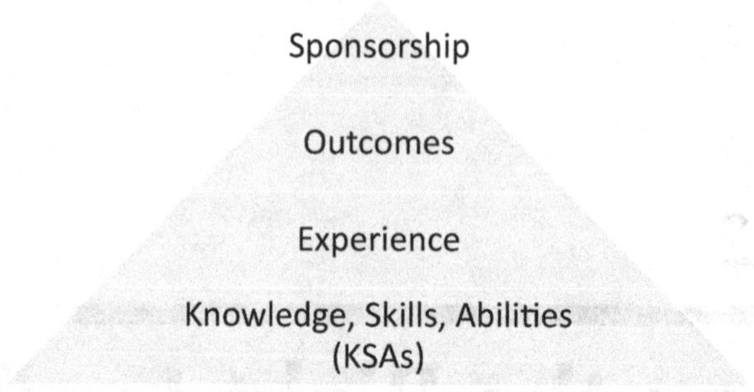

Sponsorship

Outcomes

Experience

Knowledge, Skills, Abilities
(KSAs)

Figure 2   Leadership Fundamentals.

adds value. Some experience is difficult, challenging and can be dangerous to one's career journey if not mitigated properly.

For example, mistakes are often a good teaching tool in the experience realm. When leaders make mistakes, they learn what to do and what to avoid next time. The question is will there be a next time? The risk is the degree of the mistake. If mistakes are high enough on the risk meter, they can cost leaders their jobs and/or future promotions.

Once leaders gain base KSAs and experience, the next tollgate along the journey is outcomes. It's a normal expectation for leaders to focus on the value equation for significant outcomes. Again, the focus areas will be role, organization and industry dependent. But, generic outcomes will improve service, cost and quality, as a starter.

Outcomes are predicated on leaders' abilities to manage relationships. Those that produce the greatest outcomes tend to do so as a result of influencing others along the right path. The adage of 'leading from the front' applies here. This is where leadership sponsors enter the picture.

A leadership sponsor is a leader who is committed to the advancement of another leader, typically a subordinate (1). Sponsors are crucial for leaders to reach their full potential. Those who leverage good sponsors are over 20% more likely to find next-level opportunities (1). The key is finding the right sponsor to guide one's career journey.

Leadership sponsors serve several functions. See Figure 2.1 for details.

One, they serve as a coach. When coaching is done correctly, the sponsor takes an avid interest in the leader as a whole person. The coaching process can be formal or informal. The key is for the coach to guide the leader to a better place by identifying strengths and weaknesses. Once identified, the coach assists the leader in magnifying strengths and mitigating weaknesses.

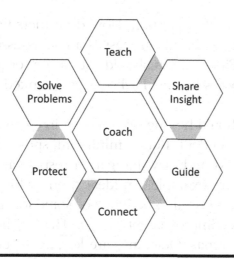

Figure 2.1   Leadership Sponsor Attributes.

Two, effective sponsors teach and share insight. Learning does not stop with formal academic programs. Leaders learn along each phase of the career journey. If not, they won't be leaders very long. The key is for sponsors to share both good and bad experiences. They also should teach their protégés technical knowledge (role dependent), operational insight related to running the business and improvement attributes such as change management. Sharing knowledge can save leaders a lot of time, stress and difficulty as they walk the path.

Third, sponsors help protect and guide up-and-coming leaders for problem resolution. Regardless of industry, leadership is a tough business. The test of one's mettle is the ability to solve problems. Leaders will find sooner rather than later that not everyone has your best interest in mind. Some colleagues are advocates, while others are detractors. This relates to the art of leadership particularly focusing on discernment.

Irrespectively, effective sponsors will protect their protégés when the waters become rough. They also will help leaders discern friend from foe. Effective sponsors have a knack for connecting leaders with the right contacts that provide the greatest probability of success long term. This discernment will also be very helpful in determining, for example, which roles to take, pass on and postpone for a later date. One of the biggest pitfalls leaders experience is pursuing a role that is not the best fit for their skill set and future career journey. The key is for sponsors to ensure leaders keep a solid footing and avoid the potholes along the career journey.

Here is the million-dollar question. How do leaders find the ideal sponsor? A simple tool to assist in this process is a risk assessment tool. See figure 2.2 for details. First, leaders should list current or potential sponsors. Then, the ranking process begins. Each leader is ranked, as noted in Figure 2.2, on several attributes.

An ideal sponsor should be one who has an integrated skill set. This skill set is industry dependent. But, at minimum, sponsors should have the 'chops' in their respective industry that garner respect and credibility. Let's use a healthcare industry example. An ideal sponsor for a healthcare leader would be one who has clinical experience of some form, operational experience and performance improvement 'chops.' The key here is significant outcomes in all three arenas. Outcomes are key, as experience in a certain field is not an indicator of success.

An ideal sponsor should also be assessed for how they interact with subordinate leaders. Do they take a vested interest in leadership growth? Have they developed formal coaching plans to help their leaders mature, grow and advance? Do they spend personal time (professionally speaking) with their leaders to understand the whole person? Do they communicate personally or prefer impersonal techniques such as e-mails or text messages?

It's also important to assess how the sponsor shares knowledge. The right sponsor can save leaders decades of learning by sharing insight. Again, the key is to connect with the right sponsor. But, the ideal sponsor is one who freely shares knowledge to grow the pie.

Let's take a practical look at Figure 2.2. A high-performing thought leader is assessing three potential sponsors. The end goal is to find the right sponsor who will help the leader reach senior executive level roles in the next 3 years. As noted in Figure 2.2, the leader ranks each sponsor separately on the attributes.

The assessment reveals a lot of positives about Sponsor 1. This sponsor is a top performer with an integrated skill set. Thus, this sponsor possesses a diversified experience portfolio and meets over 90% of their operational goals. Sponsor 1 prefers in-person communication on a regular basis and has formal plans for growth and coaching leaders. This sponsor relishes getting to know the whole person when coaching leaders and overall is an advocate for growth. As noted, Sponsor 1 is a low-risk candidate, meaning they would be a good fit for the leader.

Sponsor 2's assessment paints a slightly different picture. This sponsor does not have an integrated skill set and meets 70% to 90% of their goals. Thus, the level of organizational knowledge and subsequent outcomes are

Sponsor	Sponsor Goal Attainment 1->90% 2-70%-90% 3-<70%	Sponsor Time Commitment to You 1-Weekly 2-Monthly 3-No Time Commitment	Sponsor's Growth Plan for You 1-Formal Plan 2-Informal Plan 3-No Plan	Sponsor's Coaching Perspective 1-Formal Coaching 2-Informal Coaching 3-No Coaching	Does Sponsor Share Knowledge? 1-Yes 2-No	Does Sponsor Show Interest in You As a Whole Person? 1-Yes 2-No	Does Sponsor Have An Integrated Skill Set? 1-Yes 2-No	How Does Sponsor Communicate? 1-In Person 2-Electronically	Risk Score *Sum Columns 2-9 Lower Score = Lower Risk	Risk Level
Sponsor 1	1	1	1	1	1	1	1	1	8	Low Risk
Sponsor 2	2	2	2	2	1	1	2	2	14	Average Risk
Sponsor 3	3	3	3	3	2	2	2	2	20	High Risk

Figure 2.2   Leadership Sponsor Risk Tool.

average at best. Also, this sponsor tends to coach and grow leaders informally. Their communication style and interaction habits are different as well. Sponsor 2 prefers interactions on a monthly basis and mainly through e-mails or text messages. The adage of 'leading from afar' applies here. Overall, this sponsor is ranked as average risk. There are benefits and risks with choosing this sponsor. The reality is that the thought leader's chance of success with this sponsor is relatively similar to a coin toss. It may be good (heads), or it may not fare well (tails). This decision would be a gamble with reasonably expected benefits.

Sponsor 3 is ranked as a high-risk candidate. This simply means that the assessing leader would not be wise to select this sponsor as a first choice. Sponsor 3 is a low performer operationally and has limited organizational knowledge. This sponsor also has no formal plans to coach, mentor or grow leaders. The communication style and time commitment are also questionable. This sponsor prefers impersonal communication that is most infrequent. Simply put, this sponsor would be a shot in the dark and not the best choice for the leader with aggressive career growth plans.

Summary

What did we learn? Simply put, not all sponsors are the same. Selecting the right sponsor is a risky proposition, and risk is important. Moreover, leaders don't know what they don't measure.

As noted in the case study, sponsorship is a serious consideration. Ideal sponsors are those who take a vested interest in their leaders. The end goal is for the sponsor to accelerate their leader's maturity, growth, performance and vertical potential (i.e., promotability). From a leader perspective, we learned that discernment is key in aligning with the right sponsor.

The litmus test is simple. Does the sponsor value me as an individual and truly care about the whole person? Is the sponsor willing to make my career path a priority with adequate time investments? Does the sponsor have the insight, skills and outcomes to help advance my career? If the answer is no to these considerations, then the sponsor is likely to be high risk. Thus, leaders should look for other options.

In summary, leaders should stick to the basics when aligning with potential sponsors. The goal is for the sponsor, leader and organization as a whole to grow, mature and be more effective over time. The key to success is risk. We don't know what we don't measure. Thus, one's ability to assess, measure, analyze and mitigate risks will determine if their sponsor choice will be the biggest bang for the buck or simply a dud. The key is for leaders to measure, discern and choose wisely.

Reference

1. Leadership Research Institute. Who's Your Leadership Sponsor? A Practical Guide to Finding the Right Sponsor. www.lri.com/resources/useletter/whos-leadership-sponsor/

Chapter 3

Leadership Guide to Maximizing Career Value Potential

Why Leadership Matters

Leadership is a risky business. Merriam-Webster defines leadership as 'The capacity to lead.' Is a leader someone with an important title? Is leadership the act of leading people to a desired end? What defines leadership success? Will a title alone ensure leaders are successful long term? Are all leaders successful? Is goal attainment related to service, cost and quality the ultimate indicator of leadership success, or are other attributes required? Is it possible for leaders to experience career plateaus? Does leadership value potential matter, and can it be measured? Will the value leaders contribute to the organization and its customers increase, stagnate or decline with time? We answer these and other considerations in the rest of this chapter.

In layman's terms, leadership is getting others to do what you want without force. For years, leadership has been used interchangeably with tag lines such as relationship management, visionary, political savvy and the like. Will politics alone ensure leaders are successful long term and add value at every turn? The short answer is not anymore. Leadership is not unifocal. There are several attributes leaders must master to survive in high-risk environments. The only question is how many leaders will evolve to make the cut?

In today's world, value is the new minimum standard. Value is essentially anything the customer is willing to pay for (1). Does the customer really care

DOI: 10.4324/9781003335108-4

about someone's title or accomplishments? More than likely not. So, what is a practical perspective of value? Most leaders consider a value-add to be anything that improves service, cost and quality. Are there other value indicators, particularly for leadership? Simply put, yes.

Recently, a top thought leader was offered a promotion with a large service organization. This leader was a tenured change agent that continued to increase in knowledge, performance and knowledge sharing for their entire career. One day, the leader received an invite to the executive suite. On arrival, the leader met with a senior executive who offered the new role.

The conversation started with waves of praise by the executive for the leader's progressive performance and outcomes over many years. Within seconds, the executive shifted the conversation starkly. The executive told the leader that 'As long as you perform and get outcomes, everything will be fine.' The leader was taken aback by that statement.

What does *perform* mean? If one arrives to work on time each day, does this qualify for performing? If one sets basic goals and meets them, does this qualify one as a high performer? Is keeping a good attitude at work an indicator of performance?

What about outcomes? What outcomes meet expectations? Is this in reference to improving value to customers or just internal metrics? The takeaway was the directive was very vague, confusing and not helpful for the road ahead. The adage of 'you're only as good as your last performance' was the theme in the conversation.

The lesson learned from the conversation is simple. Leaders must understand value and their value potential. A leader's value potential is a simple concept. What is the potential for a leader to add value and continue to do so long term throughout their career?

Leadership Value Curve

Figure 3 outlines three tracts for leaders during their career as it relates to value potential. The premise is simple. Ideally, leaders should improve their outcomes over time progressively. Thus, their value potential increases over time. The greater is the value contributed, the better the organization and industry fare long term.

The ideal value tract is for leaders to add more value each year as compared to previous years. This tract is synonymous with top talent and progressive leaders. The second track is indicated by the marginal value curve.

Marginal value potential is indicated by leaders who improve outcomes initially, then plateau at some point in their career and stagnate long term. The minimal value curve is noted for those leaders who add little value at any point along the career tract. This minimal value contribution tends to remain low for the entirety of the career.

It's important to note that the leadership career journey is fluid. Along the way, leaders will experience ups and downs, good times and challenging times. But, only those who fall off the horse and get back on it will reach their ideal value potential. Persistence is key.

Leadership Disruption Lattice

In today's landscape, value is captured in various forms. Obviously, the starting point is key performance indicator (KPI) goal attainment. This traditional view of leadership value is simple. Can leaders set and meet goals that will add value to the organization and its customers? The goal is to be better each year. Thus, the value theme is progression.

Leaders will also be assessed on their value potential as it relates to knowledge and vision. Does the leader have the base knowledge for the job? Has the leader continued to learn over the course of their career and grow their knowledge base? Is the leader a knowledge sharer? Does the leader frequently publish articles or books or present in national venues to share industry knowledge?

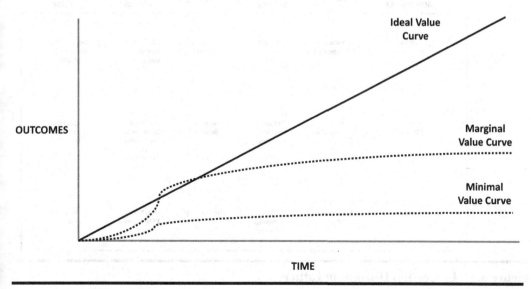

Figure 3   Leadership Value Curve.

Does the leader have a vision for the future? This vision is synonymous with strategic plan. Does the leader have a 3- to 5-year plan for their career, their operational area(s) and their people? These are just a few considerations worth noting.

Leaders' value potential will also be impacted by their ability to think innovatively. This simply entails creating new ways of doing business. Has the leader created a new model or concept that was accepted by the industry and added value in some form? Were the outcomes of this innovative concept significant? Is the model a mainstay in the industry currently?

The key is for leaders to progress and add value at every turn. But, how does one know where they stand at each stage of the journey? Are they in a good spot, standing in a pothole or driving off the cliff, operationally speaking? Figure 3.1 is a simple leadership disruption lattice. It's a tool for leaders to assess themselves and their subordinate leaders as it relates to disruption and value potential.

As noted in the figure, there are three zones. The safe zone is for higher performers. These leaders tend to have formal plans for knowledge sharing and strategic planning. They always look several years out and plan for what is ahead proactively. This zone is synonymous with the ideal value potential curve in Figure 3.

	KPI Goal Attainment	Vision	Knowledge Sharing	Learning	Integrated Skill Set	Innovative Thinking
SAFE ZONE	> 80%	Formal Strategic Plan	Formal Knowledge Sharing	Proactive Learner	Technical + Operations + Improvement Skills	Creates New Concepts & Models
CAUTION ZONE	70%–80%	Informal Strategic Plan	Informal Knowledge Sharing	Learn if Required	Technical or Operations or Improvement Skills (2 of the 3 Skills)	Adopts New Concepts & Models
DISRUPTION ZONE	<70%	No Strategic Plan	No Knowledge Sharing	No Learning	Only 1 of the 3 Skills Above	Favors Status Quo

Figure 3.1   Leadership Disruption Lattice.

They also tend to have integrated skill sets composed of technical, operational and improvement skills. Think of a healthcare executive, for example. The executive has a nursing background, years of operational leadership experience running large divisions of a health system and a Six Sigma Black Belt with significant outcomes. The key is not just experience but significant outcomes with these skills.

The safe zone is also attributed to those leaders who learn and think outside the box. The adage of 'coloring outside the lines' applies here. These leaders tend to create new ways of doing business regularly via innovative concepts and models. They also tend to be lifelong learners. They continually pursue new skills and insight to grow the industry, improve value and impact the body of knowledge for generations to come.

The second leadership disruption zone is the caution zone. This correlates with the marginal value potential curve in Figure 3. Here leaders tend to meet 70% to 80% of their operational goals with only two of the three skills sets. They tend to be reactive to learning and choose these opportunities if required.

Also, this zone is characterized by leaders who possess informal plans for knowledge sharing and strategic planning. These leaders tend to adopt best practices instead of creating them. The adage of 'armchair quarterback' applies. The key here is that leaders who find themselves in the caution zone should reevaluate their value contributions and pivot sooner rather than later.

The third leadership disruption zone is the disruption zone itself. These leaders have a high probability of not adding enough value to be successful long term. Think of great white shark hunting zones. Often, biologists refer to the kill zone geographically. In certain parts of the world, there are high numbers of great white sharks close to seal colonies. The sharks, over time, have honed their hunting tactics and attack only when a seal is in the kill zone. Thus, they have the greatest probability of success while hunting.

Leaders should think of the disruption zone the same way. It is synonymous with the minimal value curve in Figure 3. As time passes, these leaders add minimal value to the organization and its customers. Thus, their risk levels are much higher, their value never peaks and they are in deep waters operationally speaking with the greatest chance of being disrupted. The key is for these leaders to make drastic changes quickly. Otherwise, they will be disrupted sooner rather than later.

Case in Point

A large service organization was experiencing higher than normal levels of risk and disruptions. The industry was evolving, and larger organizations began to grow while their smaller counterparts were being disrupted and absorbed by competitors. The enterprise leaders realized the organization was riding the fence.

Operationally, the enterprise was strong in service, but it had challenges with cost control and revenue streams. If not corrected, the organization would be forced into a merger or acquisition. Thus, leaders and stakeholders would be disrupted.

A team of leaders realized change was needed but did not have insight as to the gravity of the current state. They used the leadership disruption lattice as part of the organizational assessment. The goal was to determine which leaders at every level were in the safe zone. Simply put, they needed to identify top performers who could lead the enterprise through a very quick turnaround.

Their presumption was that most of the leaders were top performers who resided in the safe zone. Was their perception reality? Let's see.

As noted in Figure 3.2, the enterprise used a simple risk tool to assess their top leaders.

Each leader was assessed on the value attributes previously mentioned. The results were startling. Sixty percent of the top leaders were in high-risk positions. This simply meant they resided operationally in the disruption zone. Overall, they struggled with goal attainment, skills sets, learning and creating new ways of doing business. As the industry evolved, they were at best on the marginal value curve in Figure 3.

In contrast, only 20% of the leaders were in the safe zone. This leader thrived as a top performer and mirrored the ideal value curve in Figure 3. As time passed, the leader was a visionary and learned new skills that afforded higher goal attainment. Moreover, this leader was a progressive planner as relates to strategy and knowledge sharing.

The adage of 'staying ahead of the curve' applies here. This leader was the ideal fit for the organization's turnaround, but the enterprise had one more hurdle. Can one person turn around a large organization by themselves? The short answer is no.

Leader	Integrated Skill Set 1- Technical + Operations + Improvement 2- 2 of the 3 Skill Sets 3- 1 of the 3 Skills Sets	Strategic Plan 1- Formal Plan 2- Informal Plan 3- No Plan	Knowledge Sharing 1- Formal Plan 2- Informal Plan 3- No Plan	Develop New Concepts/Models 1- Creates Models 2- Adopts Models 3- Favors Status Quo	KPI Goal Attainment 1- >80% 2- 70%-80% 3- <70%	Learning 1- Proactive Learner 2- Learn if Required 3- No Learning	Risk Score *Sum Columns 2-7 Lower Score = Lower Risk	Risk Level	Leader Value Position
Leader 1	1	1	1	1	1	1	6	Low Risk	Safe Zone
Leader 2	2	3	2	3	2	2	14	High Risk	Disruption Zone
Leader 3	2	2	2	2	3	2	13	High Risk	Disruption Zone
Leader 4	1	2	1	3	2	3	12	Average Risk	Caution Zone
Leader 5	3	3	3	3	3	3	18	High Risk	Disruption Zone
Avg Score	1.8	2.2	1.8	2.4	2.2	2.2			
Risk Level	Low Risk	High Risk	Low Risk	High Risk	High Risk	High Risk			

Figure 3.2 Leader Value Position Risk Assessment Tool.

Summary

The lesson learned from this case study is that leaders don't know what they don't measure. Leadership is a risky business. How will one know if they reside in the safe zone, caution zone or disruption zone (i.e., 'kill zone')? The simplest answer is to use a disruption lattice and risk assessment tool.

Change is the only norm in today's world. As change increases, so does risk. Risk can be leveraged for positive change if recognized early and harnessed. If leaders miss the mark in their awareness, risk will quickly become the ultimate disruptor.

We learned from the case study that perception is not always reality. The perception was that the operational issues were derived from a small group of leaders and could be quickly addressed. In reality, the organization's top leadership team was behind the eight ball and lacked in various value attributes. Thus, the enterprise was at risk of being the next acquisition from its 'Pac-Man' competitors.

In summary, leaders must realize that value matters. The adage of 'nothing earned is nothing gained' always applies. Value impacts everyone in the long run. Everyone includes the organization, leaders, staff, customers and even competitors. For leaders to remain viable and maximize their career value potential, they must plan ahead, leverage knowledge, learn continually, integrate skills and outperform the competition. If not, the leadership joy ride will quickly evolve into a plunge over the cliff.

Reference

1. Institute of Industrial and Systems Engineers (IISE), Lean Green Belt, 2016.

Chapter 4

The Risk of a Leadership Brand: Is It a Stamp of Approval or Scarlet Letter?

The Importance of Brand

Merriam-Webster defines a brand as, 'a public image, reputation, or identity conceived of as something to be marketed or promoted' or 'a mark of disgrace.' In layman's terms, a brand is the perceived value a leader adds to the organization and its stakeholders. Does a leadership brand have both upside and downside affects? The short answer is yes.

A brand can be compared to a double-edged sword. If leaders are branded as being industry leaders, experts in their field and influencers, the brand's sword will remove barriers to vertical opportunities. This is synonymous with a stamp of approval for next-level success. In contrast, if the brand is unfavorable, it can be a scarlet letter or mark of disgrace. Simply put, an unfavorable brand can hinder or cripple a leader's future if not cultivated properly.

This leads to several considerations. Does a brand really matter? Is leadership branding unifocal, or are there several levels of brand to consider? Is the leader brand journey a straight shot to the top or a process over time? Do all leaders mature their brands at the same rate and reach the same level of success? Can a brand determine a leader's tenure, influence the chance for being disrupted and provide clarity on career next steps? Is it possible to risk assess the leadership brand to determine the potential for success or failure? We answer these and other considerations in the rest of this chapter.

DOI: 10.4324/9781003335108-5

Leadership Brand Levels

A good starting point when considering a leader brand relates to levels. See Figure 4 for details.

A brand is not a one-size-fits-all model. There are several levels to consider. First, the ideal brand is an influencer. An influencer from a leadership perspective is synonymous with top talent. These leaders tend to be industry leaders, master change agents and model or champion industry best practices. They are the 'go-to' for all the organization's gnarly challenges. Influencers also tend to be top performers and lead organizational outcomes even in the most challenging circumstances.

The second level of leadership brand is contributor. This level is synonymous with one who adds higher levels of value to the organization and its stakeholders. This leader type tends to be a higher performer in attributes such as service, cost and quality. They contribute to long-term organizational success and add higher levels of value in organizational outcomes. The goal is to elevate contributors to the influencer level.

The third level of brand is the backbone. Backbone leaders tend to represent the majority of organizations. They are the oil that greases the skids, operationally speaking. These backbone leaders tend to add required value

Brand Level	Common Synonym	Attributes
Influencer	Top Talent	• Industry leader • Master change agent • Model/Champion best practices • Top performer • Lead organizational outcomes
Contributor	Higher Value	• Contribute to organizational success • Add higher levels of value in organizational outcomes
Back Bone	Value Add	• Bearers of organizational culture • Ensure day-to-day business runs as intended
Follower	Improvement Needed	• Member of the pack • Go along to get along • Reactive approach to organizational success
Anchor	Unsatisfactory	• Take more than give • Detractor of organizational success, higher performance and forward progress • Apathetic to organizational success

Figure 4   Leadership Brand Levels.

at every turn. They also are the bearers of organizational culture, norms and the way work gets done. In short, they ensure the business runs day to day as intended. Without this subgroup, the organization would cease to exist.

The fourth level of leadership branding relates to followers. Followers are often compared to those that add minimal value and need to improve performance. They tend to be a member of the pack, go along to get along and are more reactive in their approach to organizational success. The adage of 'bare minimum performance' applies here. The goal is for the organization to incentivize this subgroup to perform better or look for employment options outside the organization.

The last level of leadership branding is the anchor. Organizational anchors are often referred to as those leaders who add no value to the organization. They tend to take more than they give. Also, they are detractors or apathetic to the organization's long-term success and forward progress. The key here is to purge this subgroup from the enterprise.

Leadership Brand Journey Map

Along with brand levels, leaders must consider the leadership brand journey. Leadership branding is a journey that follows leaders their entire career. See Figure 4.1 for details.

One's brand typically starts at the beginner phase. This occurs when leaders enter the organization or industry. The adage 'fish out of water' applies here. The beginner phase occurs when leaders are becoming acquainted with the basics of leading others. These attributes include learning the basics of a job such as showing up on time, completing assignments on time and correctly and the like. The focus is showing one is dependable, trustworthy, competent in basic tasks and has potential to do more.

The next phase of branding is synonymous with learning. It typically occurs in tandem with the beginner phase. In short, here leaders learn the basics of a leadership role such as base knowledge, skills and abilities to succeed. Credential building is the main focus during this time. They also learn organizational values, norms and the political landscape. Great insight is gained as to how the organization works and who the power brokers are.

As leaders mature, their brand enters the higher performer phase. Here leaders use the basics to produce noticeable outcomes. These outcomes often spill over to other areas, and these cross-functional wins elevate the brand like a rocket ship. This phase in branding is the catalyst to next-level opportunities and career shaping for senior leadership roles. What is

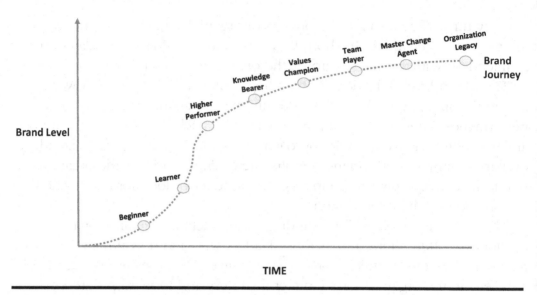

Figure 4.1   Leadership Brand Journey Map.

accomplished here will follow the leader for many years. This is where the stamp of approval or scarlet letter emerge.

The next phase of branding is becoming a knowledge bearer. It's important to note that knowledge comes with time and through experience. One of the biggest mistakes leaders make is assuming academic training fully prepares them for leadership success. Academics can be compared to tires on a car. They simply help the car move forward. But, fuel and other mechanical parts are needed for a long, successful journey.

The key with branding related to knowledge is that it is twofold. One aspect is organizational knowledge. This simply relates to how the organization runs day to day and the right way to do work. It takes years working in various roles and different areas to amass a respectable cache of organizational knowledge. In contrast, the other aspect of knowledge relates to the industry (i.e., external knowledge). Once leaders establish themselves as organizational leaders, they must then begin learning a much bigger picture. The adage 'small fish in a big pond' applies here. The organizational knowledge is just the beginning step to branding one as an industry leader. More work, time and accomplishments are needed externally to be considered an industry leader.

Once leaders are recognized as knowledge bearers, they evolve into values champions. This phase of branding includes higher levels of emotional intelligence. Leaders learn here how to lead by example, lead others through change and get others to do what they want without force. The art of leadership comes to light here. Those who are successful in this phase will move forward. Those who stumble will not progress.

As leaders master values and organizational norms, they then transition into the team player brand. Here other leaders perceive the leader to be one who can improve other teams. The greater the value perceived from a leader's brand, the bigger the doors that will open. The key here is growing the pie and adding value to others. This phase in leadership branding involves a growing awareness of empathy, synergy and avoiding groupthink.

Once leaders master the art of team, they evolve to the master change agent brand. This brand is unique and not easily attainable. The master change agent is one who can go anywhere at any time and lead cross-functional teams to the promised land, operationally speaking. Simply put, this brand is a master influencer and results getter. They thrive in any environment. Think of a Navy SEAL, organizationally speaking.

Finally, leaders evolve into becoming part of the organization's legacy. Here leaders are branded as irreplaceable fixtures in the organization and industry as a whole. At this phase in the career journey, leaders focus on leaving a legacy on the industry and ensuring future generations will be best prepared to carry the torch. These leaders' time is scarce and very valuable. Thus, their contributions are highly regarded.

Leadership Brand Maturity Curve

As one progresses along the career journey, their brand can follow different tracks. See Figure 4.2 for examples.

The end goal is for leaders to increase their brand, political capital and effectiveness over time. Top performers who are seen as adding higher levels of value and leading the industry tend to follow the ideal brand curve.

As these leaders progress from beginners to master change agents, their brands progressively mature. They become more valuable to the organization, industry and other industries over time. Also, these leaders have higher levels of political capital and effectiveness with time. The adage 'mover and shaker' applies here.

In contrast, leaders whose brands stumble along the journey may follow the minimal brand curve. Here leaders achieve only minimal levels of political capital and effectiveness during the course of a career. They quickly evolve into followers or less as noted in Figure 4. Organizations should invest thought, time and resources to help these leaders with branding, outcomes

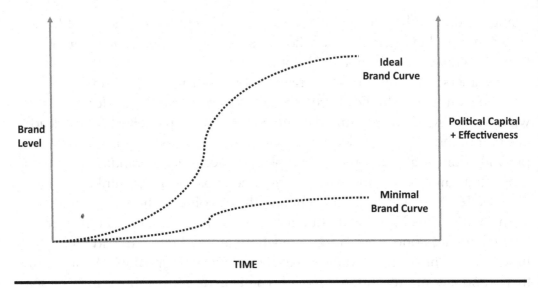

Figure 4.2   Leadership Brand Maturity Curve.

and the journey. Otherwise, these leaders will be minimally effective. Thus, the organization and its stakeholders will experience lesser value over time.

Leadership Brand Disruption Lattice

One key aspect of leadership branding is determining where one fits on the disruption lattice. Simply put, is the leader's brand safe, at risk for disruption or is disruption imminent? See Figure 4.3 for details.

As noted in Figure 4.3, leadership branding has three zones based on several attributes as discussed previously. Leaders whose brand is safe or low risk tend to be higher performers in change, knowledge and outcomes. Simply put, they outperform the rest of the pack. They also tend to champion organizational values, sponsor change and master the art of team building. These top performers have a safe or low-risk brand as they add the greatest value to the organization, stakeholders and industry as a whole. This zone is synonymous with influencers as previously noted.

The caution zone simply means leaders are at risk based on their brands. There is an opportunity to recover and pivot to the safe zone. But, these leaders tend to be average in goal attainment and knowledge. They also participate in team activities and change initiatives instead of leading them. Also, they support instead of champion organizational values. The key here is these leaders tend to follow instead of lead and must change. Otherwise,

	KPI Goal Attainment	Values	Organizational Knowledge	Team Player	Change Agent
SAFE ZONE	> 80%	Champion Values	High (Knowledge Bearer)	Sponsor Teams	Champion Change
CAUTION ZONE	70%-80%	Support Values	Medium (Learner)	Participate in Teams	Support Change
DISRUPTION ZONE	<70%	Go It Alone	Low (Lacking Knowledge)	Go It Alone	Resist or Neutral to Change

Figure 4.3   Leadership Brand Disruption Lattice.

disruption is a forthcoming reality as they are perceived to contribute minimal levels of value at best.

Finally, the disruption zone is simply that—highly disruptive. In this zone, leaders are perceived to resist change and go it alone versus value the team approach. Also, they have limited organizational or industry knowledge accompanied with lower goal attainment. They also are perceived as late adopters to change instead of front-runners. The key here is that these leaders are at imminent or high risk of being disrupted. Moreover, the organization is also in a risky position as these leaders are synonymous with anchors as noted in Figure 4.

Case in Point

You may be wondering what this all means. Is leadership branding really important? Let's take a closer look at a real example of how risk impacts the brand.

A large service organization began the journey toward higher levels of performance. This journey had both internal and external drivers. Internally, the organization had experienced several years of operational declines in service, costs and quality, for example. Top leaders realized a new path forward was warranted operationally. But, which path to take was a point of contention.

The other driver was external. Market forces began to swirl causing higher than normal disruption levels. The industry began to experience significant downturns in revenue with higher than expected cost trends. The result was record-level mergers and acquisitions never seen before. Organizational insolvency became the norm for most enterprises. The organization was at a crossroads of being able to continue to stand alone versus seeking a larger partner to provide needed resources and economies of scale.

The enterprise's goal was to leverage the current top leadership team as a conduit to weather the storm and conduct an operational turnaround. The first phase included an organizational assessment. The perception was that the top leadership cadre was high performing and comprised several industry leaders. Again, this was a perception viewed through a single lens.

As part of the assessment, an external executive coach was engaged to conduct an objective analysis of the team's brand, performance potential and value added. The coach used a simple risk assessment tool to provide insight never seen before for each leader on the team. See Figure 4.4 for details.

Each leader was assessed on various attributes as noted in Figure 4.3. Was the leader a team player who championed values? Did the leader actually lead change initiatives or follow the crowd and accept the status quo? Was the leader a knowledge bearer or one with limited organizational and industry knowledge? Finally, the leaders were scored on their operational goal attainment tied to service, cost and quality contributions. The tool provided an objective lens of the current state risk for each leader and their actual versus perceived contributions to the organization and beyond.

The coach completed the assessment and presented the results as noted in Figure 4.4 to the enterprise leaders. The reality was surprising to say the least. Only 40% of the top leaders were influencers. These leaders were organization and industry leaders of change. They also produced better outcomes than their peers because of bearing more knowledge, skills and abilities. Thus, they resided in the safe zone related to their brand and were low risk to the organization.

In contrast, 60% of the top leaders were at best in the caution zone. Forty percent of those leaders were in the disruption zone. Think of a group of Air Force bombers approaching a target. They focus their bomb drop on the target. These 40% were theoretically standing in the bull's-eye of the drop zone. They were high risk to the organization and were directly responsible for the organization's operational issues.

The reality is that perception was not reality in this scenario. The leadership brand of the top team was majority high risk and favorably disposed to

Leader	Team Player 1- Sponsor Teams 2- Participate in Teams 3- Go It Alone	Values 1- Champion Values 2- Support Values 3- Ignore Values	Knowledge Level 1- Knowledge Bearer 2- Learner 3- Novice	Change Agent 1- Champion Change 2- Support Change 3- Resist Change	KPI Goal Attainment 1- >80% 2- 70%-80% 3- <70%	Risk Score *Sum Columns 2-6 Lower Score = Lower Risk	Risk Level	Leader Brand Position
Leader 1	1	1	1	1	1	5	Low Risk	Safe Zone
Leader 2	2	3	2	3	2	12	High Risk	Disruption Zone
Leader 3	2	2	2	2	2	10	Average Risk	Caution Zone
Leader 4	1	2	1	3	2	9	Low Risk	Safe Zone
Leader 5	3	3	3	3	3	15	High Risk	Disruption Zone

Avg Score
Risk Level

	Team Player	Values	Knowledge Level	Change Agent	KPI Goal Attainment
Avg Score	1.8	2.2	1.8	2.4	2.0
Risk Level	Low Risk	High Risk	Low Risk	High Risk	Low Risk

Low Risk 5
Max Risk 15
Avg Risk 10

Figure 4.4   Leader Brand Risk Assessment Tool.

being disrupted. Thus, the enterprise's plan could not include all the current leaders to lead the turnaround. The challenge was that the low-risk and highly branded leaders were too few in number to turn around the organization by themselves. The adage 'a day late and a dollar short' applies here.

Summary

The reality is that leaders don't know what they don't measure. Perception is not always reality. Leaders often don't measure key attributes until it's too late as in the case study previously noted. Often, ignorance is perceived as bliss. But in reality, ignorance is high risk to organizations and never bliss. Thus, what leaders and their organizations don't know will eventually hurt them at the least opportune time.

We learned that a brand really does matter. If the brand is relevant to the current state, it can influence change, outcomes and forward progress positively. If the brand is perception only or misperceived, leaders and their organizations may be disrupted by high levels of risk sooner rather than later. The key is discerning fact from fiction.

In summary, leadership brands are multifocal and can be complicated. Creating, cultivating and magnifying a brand is a journey that must be well thought out. The leader brand journey is not a straight shot to the top. It's more of a process over time with many tollgates.

Unfortunately, all leaders will not mature their brands at the same rate and reach the same level of success. The key is to ensure leader contributions are of value, progress over time and grow the pie to improve others. In short, effective leaders and organizations are those that ensure brands are realistically a stamp of approval instead of a scarlet letter. How is this achieved? Ensure one's brand is low risk and that it always resides in the disruption safe zone.

Chapter 5

The Risk of Investing Time

Importance of Time

Per Merriam-Webster, time can be defined as, 'An appointed, fixed, or customary moment or hour for something to happen, begin, or end.' In layman's terms, time is synonymous with a period, moment, dimension or phase and the like. The key is that time is finite. This means we are given a limited span of time in life. Once it's gone, we don't get it back. Thus, we must use our time wisely.

Moreover, time has boundaries. Activities start and stop. These guardrails of time provide windows of opportunity for leaders to create and add value personally and professionally. The question is how many leaders use their time wisely? Do they realize time is being wasted before it's too late? Once a day is gone, we simply don't get it back. Therefore, leaders must understand, magnify and efficiently use each minute of time in their favor.

Is time the most valuable resource we have? Is it possible to spend time well or waste it? Are there multiple dimensions of time? Do leaders take the time to analyze how much time they spend on various activities? As a leader, should the value we create increase over time? Is it possible to become stagnant as a leader and add very little value in the long run? Is investing time in activities a risky proposition? Do leaders know when their time allocations are high, medium or low risk for disruption? Will a simple risk assessment tool predict the risk of investing time in various activities? We answer these and other considerations in the sections that follow.

Let's take a closer look.

DOI: 10.4324/9781003335108-6

Dimensions of Time

The reality is that time has several dimensions worth noting. See Figure 5 for details.

First, leaders spend or should spend time daily on wellness. Wellness time encompasses the normal sleep cycle, rest, exercise and healthy lifestyle choices. The key here is that we all must sleep at some point to function. The other wellness choices vary from one person to the next.

Second, leaders spend time on growth. For this conversation, let's focus on the professional side of life. Growth includes attributes such as learning, education, upskilling as times dictate and using this knowledge to drive significant outcomes. The focus here is on equipping one with knowledge, skills and abilities to successfully lead. As times change, so must knowledge bases. Thus, growth is a continual process that never ends. It only evolves with time.

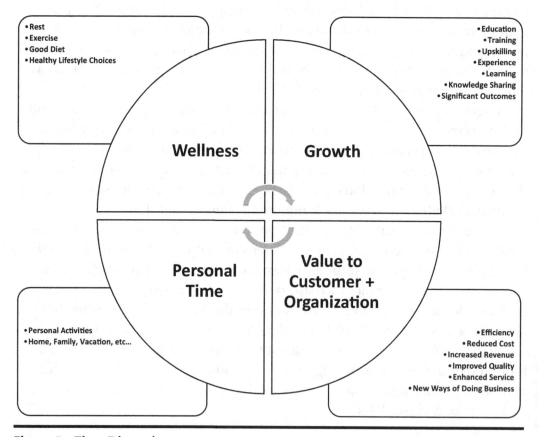

Figure 5   Time Dimensions.

Third, leaders spend a significant portion of their time adding value to stakeholders. These stakeholders include the organization and customers. Customer is synonymous with stakeholder. It's imperative for leaders to know who their customers are and what they desire. Otherwise, it's nearly impossible to add value from this perspective.

Fourth, leaders spend a portion of their time on personal time. Personal activities help balance the stress and time commitments of rigorous work routines. The focal points here tend to be maximizing value at home with family or on vacations. The adage of 'rest and relaxation' applies here.

For years, many pundits espoused the idea that the average adult spends roughly a third of life sleeping, a third of life working and a third of life in personal activities (1). These distributions of time vary from one person to another. But, the real question is how many leaders know what percentage of their time is spent on adding value to the various dimensions of time as noted in Figure 5?

Time Study Example

Let's take a practical look at a time study example. In Figure 5.1, there are three scenarios worth discussing.

Scenario 1

Dimension	Daily Time Commitment (Hrs)	% of Total Time	Annual Time Commitment (Hrs)	30 Year Career Time Commitment (Hrs)
Wellness	9	38%	2250	67500
Personal Time	7	29%	1750	52500
Growth + Value to Customer & Organization	8	33%	2000	60000
Total Hours Per Day	24			

Scenario 2

Dimension	Daily Time Commitment (Hrs)	% of Total Time	Annual Time Commitment (Hrs)	30 Year Career Time Commitment (Hrs)
Wellness	9	38%	2250	67500
Personal Time	5	21%	1250	37500
Growth + Value to Customer & Organization	10	42%	2500	75000
Total Hours Per Day	24			

Scenario 3

Dimension	Daily Time Commitment (Hrs)	% of Total Time	Annual Time Commitment (Hrs)	30 Year Career Time Commitment (Hrs)
Wellness	9	38%	2250	67500
Personal Time	3	13%	750	22500
Growth + Value to Customer & Organization	12	50%	3000	90000
Total Hours Per Day	24			

Figure 5.1   Time Study Example.

Scenario 1 outlines the time commitments of an average leader to wellness, personal time and professional activities such as growth and value. In this scenario, the leader works a typical 8-hour day. Also, 9 hours is dedicated to wellness (8 hours sleeping plus 1 hour of exercise). This leaves 7 hours per workday for personal time.

If this pattern is followed consistently, the leader would spend 38% of their time on wellness, 29% of time personally and 33% on professional activities. Over the course of a 30-year career, the leader would spend tens of thousands of hours on all three dimensions of time as noted in the figure. The real question relates to how many leaders sustain an 8-hour workday and have the discipline to maintain the other time distributions?

Scenario 2 outlines a leader's time commitment that starts with a 10-hour workday. While maintaining the dedicated 9 hours per day to wellness, this leaves 5 hours per day for personal time. If this pattern is followed, 42% of the time is spent working and only 21% is allocated for personal time. Thus, the leader would spend twice as much time on professional activities as time spent on personal attributes.

Scenario 3 outlines a more aggressive work schedule. This leader dedicates 12 hours per day working which leaves only 3 hours per day for personal time. In the long run, the leader would spend 37% more of their time working instead of focusing on personal activities. If wellness time is constant across all scenarios, the more leaders work, the less time they have for fun and basic life activities.

Why did we run through this simple example? To revisit the opening remarks saying that, time is a valuable resource, and it is finite. When time commitments are skewed on certain activities, other areas will be neglected. The takeaway is that time must be rationed. Leaders will have to determine what basic elements professionally and personally need the greatest allotment of time. If allotments of time become unbalanced and unhealthy, this will definitely impact the leader's ability to perform, add value and succeed long term. Thus, risk of investing time should be considered, weighed and mitigated at every turn.

Time Journey Map

To help leaders better understand time commitments along the career path, let's briefly discuss Figure 5.2.

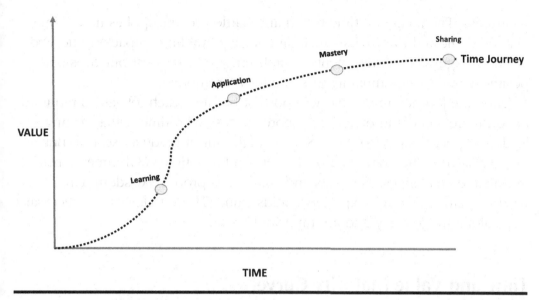

Figure 5.2   Time Journey Map: Leader Career Phases.

Figure 5.2 is a sample time journey map during various phases of one's career. The premise is that as time commitments grow over time, leaders mature in their roles. Thus, the value they add increases over time.

As noted, there are four phases in the career time journey. These tollgates relate to time commitments or windows leaders must invest in to add more value with time. Phase one is the learning phase. Every leader must start somewhere. This initial phase is where leaders gain basic training, skills and knowledge to perform certain tasks. In this phase, the basic work ethic, role integrity and trust begin to emerge with colleagues and subordinates. The learning phase is equivalent to the farmer planting a crop. Preparation is the key here.

Phase two is where this knowledge and skills are applied. Leaders begin to see the fruit of their labor. In the farmer example, this is where the harvest begins. If leaders learned and applied the knowledge properly, they will begin to add more value to the organization and customers alike. These outcomes should be tangible, measurable and significant.

Phase three of the career journey is evidenced by time committed to mastering skills. Here leaders become seasoned in their roles and professions. They begin to evolve into higher levels of expertise. Thus, the value and outcomes achieved tend to grow over time.

The final phase of the journey is noted by time leaders spend sharing knowledge, experience and talent. Here leaders have a vetted track record of success. The adage of 'time-tested and battle-proven' applies here. Time may be dedicated to activities including legacy building, impacting the body of knowledge with achievements, establishing industry best practices and positively impacting humanity in some form or another.

The time journey map is very important because each tollgate is required to add more value and experience more success with time. Often, young leaders expect to jump to the C-Suite straight out of graduate school. But in their naivete, they don't realize leadership takes time. With time comes testing and challenges. The tests and challenges produce wisdom. Finally, wisdom gained through experience adds value. These tollgates are necessary steps along the journey and are time well spent.

Time and Value Maturity Curve

To accompany the time journey map during one's career, let's look at a couple scenarios displayed in Figure 5.3.

Figure 5.3 outlines two track projections of one's time commitment and expected end. Again, time is finite and must be allocated judiciously to provide maximum value over time. Thus, leaders must choose how they spend their time wisely.

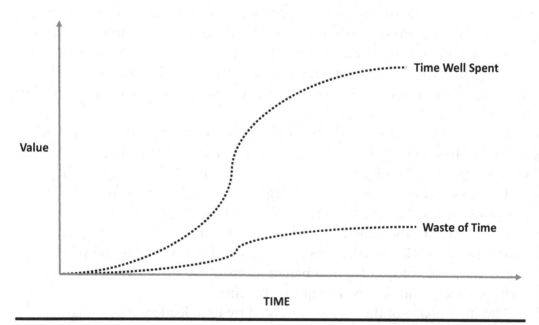

Figure 5.3 Time and Value Maturity Curve.

Track one indicates time well spent. Initially, the leader invests time in activities such as learning, applying knowledge and achieving outcomes. As time passes, time commitments should increase the value to the organization and stakeholders. The end goal is to be better, produce more and evolve over time. As noted in the time-well-spent curve, there is no resting place or vacation tollgate. Effective leaders must constantly evolve, adapt to change and find new ways of doing business.

The second track represents time wasted. The leader begins the journey with the best of intentions but along the way stagnates. Typically, leaders who achieve minimal value over time struggle with the tollgates in Figure 5.2. Far too often, leaders become career learners and don't adequately apply the knowledge to achieve significant outcomes. Taking classes for the plaque on the wall is the primary driver. The question here is how many customers are willing to pay leaders to learn if benefits are not realized from the learning? The short answer is not many.

In summary, the purpose of Figure 5.3 is to note that time is finite and must be used wisely. The career journey has a beginning and an end. No one has a forever clock. If leaders fail to produce progressively better value along the journey and mature with time, they will stagnate and face career disruptions along the way.

The key here is legacy building. At the end of one's career, what will be the story line? Leader 'x' spent time wisely that added great value to many or that time was greatly wasted. The end goal is to mature with time and add value at every turn.

Leadership Time Disruption Lattice

Another view of time relates to risk. Figure 5.4 is a simple tool for leaders to determine if the time spent professionally is on target or needs adjustment.

There are three zones in the leadership time commitment disruption lattice, and each denotes a level of risk worth considering. When time is committed, there is a risk of it being well spent or wasted. The goal is for leaders to use time wisely and maximize value, thus remaining viable and mature in outcomes with time. The safe zone is the best place to be along the career journey as it relates to the lowest risk of being disrupted.

In Figure 5.4, leaders are assessed on four attributes: measurable outcomes, growth, value to customers and value to the organization. The key here is to determine what each leader did with their time. Those who learn,

	Produce Measurable Outcomes	Growth	Value to Customers	Value to the Organization
SAFE ZONE	> 90% of the time	> 90% of the time	> 90% of the time	> 90% of the time
CAUTION ZONE	70%-90% of the time	70%-90% of the time	70%-90% of the time	70%-90% of the time
DISRUPTION ZONE	< 70% of the time	< 70% of the time	< 70% of the time	< 70% of the time

Figure 5.4   Leadership Time Disruption Lattice.

apply and master skill sets should produce measurable outcomes at least 90% of the time. If one dedicates time to improving quality, for example, and only meets goals 50% of the time, then this is a waste of time.

In terms of growth, leaders should strive to grow in skills, knowledge, experience and the like that produce significant outcomes 90% of the time or greater. The same premise is for value added from time commitments. Leaders who can realize measurable improvements 90% of the time or more tend to stay safe and are less risky to the organization and its customers.

In contrast, those leaders who struggle to grow, add value and produce outcomes 70% to 90% of the time are in the caution zone. This zone resonates with moderate risk levels. Leaders here should pivot quickly and find the safe haven with wiser time commitments that produce better outcomes.

The last zone is the disruption zone. Leaders here tend to spend their time least wisely. They struggle to meet goals or add value from their knowledge bases at least 70% of the time. Thus, they are high-risk leaders and are positioned in the disruption zone. If changes are not made quickly, value added by this leadership cadre will stagnate at best and potentially decline. They will more than likely follow the wasted time curve in Figure 4.

What's the point? There are two perspectives. One, organizations invest time and resources in leaders to get a return. The end goal is to maximize the return on investment. Leaders that are in the safe zone perform better, add more value, get better with time and provide a better return. Thus, the enterprise would invest the most time and resources here.

Two, leaders spend time making themselves and others better. This occurs with time commitments in learning, applying knowledge and producing outcomes. As time shifts from one dimension to another, leaders lose time in certain arenas. Therefore, top-performing and effective leaders are those who reside in the safe zone. Moreover, they will face the least amount of risk to their careers and livelihoods, generally speaking, over time.

The key is that organizations and their leaders don't know what they don't measure. Time matters, and how time is spent can provide a high return or result in waste.

Time Risk Assessment Tool

Finally, leaders and organizations should consider a time risk assessment tool to determine the return on time investments. See Figure 5.5 for details.

In this example, a leader completes a retrospective analysis of time spent on various activities. An organization is reviewing time commitments of various groups of leaders. The goal is to determine why some leaders produce better outcomes than their counterparts with the same resources. The adage of the aim being off target applies here.

The first step is to list the activities in question. Next, the leader scores each activity on the attributes previously noted. These attributes include value, growth and outcomes. In the figure, only 40% of the activities are a good use of time, and 60% are a waste of time. Is the leader's time well spent? The short answer is not really. Thus, it's imperative for organizations and their leaders to determine what leaders spend time on, if the time adds value or if time is wasted. The key here is for the leader to shift time to those activities that are least risky and a good use of time.

Summary

The takeaway is that time is finite, complex and multidimensional. Time is arguably the most valuable resource we have. Time can be spent wisely or wasted. It all depends on insight and measurement. Leaders don't know what they don't measure. Moreover, ignorance is never bliss.

Activity	Does the activity add value to the customer? 1- >90% 2-70%-90% 3- <70%	Does the activity add value to the organization? 1- >90% 2-70%-90% 3- <70%	Does the activity produce measurable outcomes tied to value? 1- >90% 2-70%-90% 3- <70%	Does the activity grow the leader? 1- >90% 2-70%-90% 3- <70%	Risk Score *Sum Columns 2-5 Lower Score = Lower Risk	Risk Level	Use of Time Potential
Activity 1	1	1	1	1	4	Low Risk	Good Use of Time
Activity 2	3	3	2	3	11	High Risk	Waste of Time
Activity 3	2	2	2	2	8	Average Risk	Waste of Time
Activity 4	3	3	3	3	12	High Risk	Waste of Time
Activity 5	2	2	1	2	7	Low Risk	Good Use of Time
Avg Score	2.2	2.2	1.8	2.2			
Risk Level	High Risk	High Risk	Low Risk	High Risk			

Max Risk	12
Lowest Risk	4
Avg Risk	8

Figure 5.5   Time Risk Assessment Tool.

What leaders and their organizations don't know will eventually hurt them in some form over time. The key to using time wisely is knowing how time is spent, measuring outcomes of the time commitments and ensuring the end justifies the means. High-risk leaders, as related to growth, outcomes and value added, have a greater chance of wasting time. In contrast, their counterparts are master timekeepers to ensure they make the most of time allotted.

If leaders learn, apply knowledge, realize outcomes and share knowledge, they will make the most of their time over a career. If not, the time will be wasted with minimal value added to customers and organizations. Thus, the risk of investing time should be considered, weighed and mitigated at every turn.

In summary, time is always of the essence. Effective leaders are those who can identify, analyze, mitigate and leverage risks of time commitments wisely.

Reference

1. The Association of the 24-Hour Distribution of Time Spent in Physical Activity, Work, and Sleep with Emotional Exhaustion. *International Journal of Environmental Research and Public Health*, 2018.

Chapter 6

Is Variation High-Risk Poker or a Sure Bet?

Variation

Merriam-Webster defines variation as 'The extent to which or the range in which a thing varies.' In layman's terms, variation is simply deviation from the norm. Is variation a risky proposition? Can variation be controlled with standard work? Are there different dimensions of variation leaders should consider? Is there a journey leaders will need to travel in order to address variation and its spillover effects? Is it possible to risk assess variation and predict its impact potential on business units, people and organizations? Should leaders be reactive or proactive in addressing variation in strategy, operations and people functions? Let's take a closer look to find out.

Recently, a large service organization with several business units experienced a progressive decline in operational outcomes. The enterprise collectively impacted hundreds of thousands of customers and stakeholders annually. It also served a large geographic area with diverse populations, needs and resources bases. Over a 5-year period, the enterprise realized a 30% decline in operational outcomes tied to service, cost and quality. The impact was hundreds of millions of dollars.

This trend was a stark difference from historical performance. Traditionally, the organization was a trendsetter and best practice site for the industry. As time progressed, the industry and organization evolved. The industry

DOI: 10.4324/9781003335108-7

51

moved to a transformational landscape composed of radical change, agility and technology-driven services that never existed before. Innovative thinking quickly began to trump the incremental improvement models of years past.

Unfortunately, the organization could not keep pace. As the market and industry moved forward, the organization began to slip backward down the operational hill. Inefficiencies began to appear around every corner. Waves of leader transitions occurred in hopes of bringing in fresh new talent that could correct the organizational downturn. But, regardless of the improvement efforts, operations continued to decline.

The senior leadership team assembled a group as a last-ditch effort for a turnaround. During an initial meeting, the top leaders displayed data, graphs, trends and risk levels in various forms. Each business unit was performing at a different level with different goal attainment. Some were good, some average and some very bad.

Moreover, structures for all the business units varied greatly. Some units had Lean Six Sigma-trained resources to help with waste and inefficiencies, while others did not. In further review, planning was a burning issue. Some of the business units had formal plans for strategic planning, for example, while others did not.

The theme of the meeting unknowingly was variation. Everyone was doing many things, but everything was being done differently. The variation was acting like sugar in a car's gas tank. The car ran well for a while and then slowed. With time, the sugar rendered the engine inoperable. The same story appeared here in the top leadership meeting.

In the back of the room, a forward-thinking thought leader interjected into the conversation. In this meeting, this leader's role was to be a fly on the wall. After rounds of discussions that were fruitless, the thought leader said simply, 'The issue is simple, variation across the enterprise is causing the issues.' One could have heard a pin drop.

Most leaders failed to understand what this meant. So, more information was presented by the thought leader to the group. The intent was clarity on variation, its impact on the organization and the risks its imposes on operational efficiencies. Simply put, variation was decaying the organization from the inside out.

In short, variation is a risky proposition. Leaders need insight to determine if variation is high-risk poker or a sure bet. Let's take a closer look at a few practical examples.

Dimensions of Variation

As the thought leader shared with the group of top leaders, there are four basic dimensions of variation that leaders should consider. See Figure 6 for details.

The first dimension relates to plans. Planning is one of the most critical steps leaders and organizations will invest time, resources and knowledge in. Planning includes at minimum plans related to strategy, change, knowledge and communications.

For a brief overview, strategic plans should contain four parts at minimum. The first part of planning strategically is the assessment. This step has two perspectives: internal and external. The key here is for leaders to assess what is working, assess what is not working and identify forthcoming disruptors and the like from inside and outside the organization.

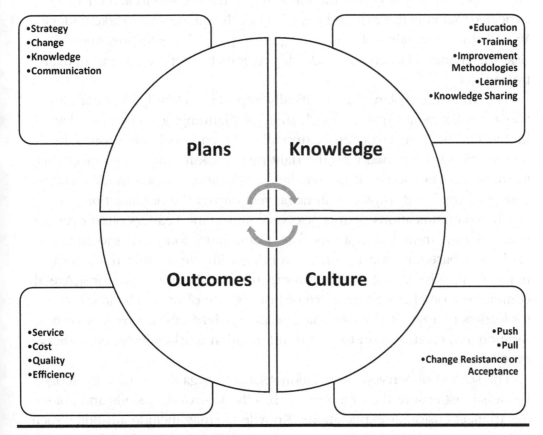

Figure 6   Dimensions of Variation.

The second part of strategy planning is where decisions are made. Here leaders select goals, create service line playbooks, set budgets and create the vision for the organization's future direction. The key is to ensure goals are tied to gaps. Moreover, goals must be correlated to budget planning to ensure resources will be available to achieve goals. Also, leaders must ensure the goals are achieved. Otherwise, the planning and resource allocation was for naught.

The next two steps in strategy planning include implementing the plan and reassessing its effectiveness. In short, there is nothing worse than doing something for the sake of just doing it. Once implemented, strategic plans should produce the desired outcomes and move the organization forward. If not, course correction is warranted.

Change plans are exactly how they sound. Leaders must have simple plans in place to successfully maneuver change. Since change is the new norm in today's world, leaders must evolve into master change agents. The change plan simply answers the following: What organizational changes are expected? What is the risk and benefit of each change to all stakeholders? What is the probability of each change disrupting the enterprise? For each risk, the change plan entails leadership actions to prepare for and mitigate those risks.

The knowledge plan is also critically important. Here leaders plan for talent management. Again, as with strategic planning, leaders must view knowledge both internally and externally. The end goal is to ensure the organization is equipped with the right people, skills, talent and mechanisms to share this knowledge. If knowledge is lacking or housed in silos, change and other market disruptors will negatively impact the organization.

The communications plan is also very important. Leaders often overlook this type of planning until it's too late. Communication plans should also take a risk-based approach. What's working with the organization's communication? What is not working in organizational communications? Are all communication channels effective or just a waste of time? The key here is for leaders to assess the current landscape, analyze effectiveness of communication and create a plan to ensure information reaches intended audiences every time.

The second dimension of variation relates to organizational knowledge. Leaders must ensure the organization has the knowledge, skills and abilities to meet customer expectations. Knowledge may include attributes such as learning, training, upskilling, adopting improvement methodologies and the like. The key is for organizations to improve knowledge over time.

Moreover, leaders must ensure the knowledge portfolio results in desired operational outcomes. Otherwise, it's training for the sake of training.

The third variation dimension is culture. Culture is simply the way work gets done. Organizational culture is composed of various people types, worldviews and ways of doing work. If leaders are not careful, the cultural differences can result in operational variation that will sink the ship. The key here is alignment of talent to ensure everyone is focused on the desired end.

The final dimension of variation is outcomes. The key here is to ensure the enterprise and its respective business units provide value to customers each and every time. Value typically emerges from attributes such as service, cost, quality and efficiency to start. Irrespective of the key performance indicator (KPI), value is simply what a customer is willing to pay for (1). Leaders must ensure that all business units perform at or above goal for the chosen KPIs. Otherwise, variation will emerge, and operational decline will soon follow.

The Journey

The thought leader then shared a simple journey map related to variation and improvement with the leadership cadre. See Figure 6.1 for details.

The key here is that organizations must chart a journey to predict, identify, minimize and ultimately harness variation. The kryptonite for variation

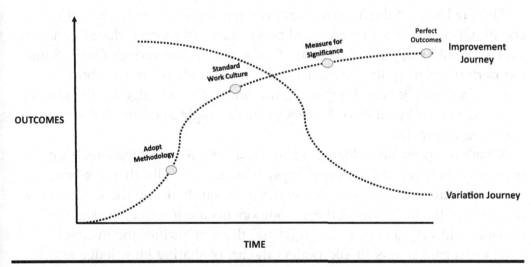

Figure 6.1 Improvement and Variation Journey Map.

is the improvement journey displayed in Figure 6.1. Organizations first adopt improvement methodologies. There are many to choose from, but many organizations choose Lean or Six Sigma and then add others, if needed, later.

Once the organization is trained and proficient with the methodology of choice, leaders must begin the standard work phase. Standard work is as it applies—simply stated, standardizing all aspects of how work gets done. The key is for leaders to focus on process. For starters, organizational processes should be captured and standardized in policies or work instructions, for example. The premise is to ensure the organizational knowledge is accurate, current, standardized and accessible to end users in real time when needed. This will ensure work is done correctly and the same every time.

Standard work also applies to data, goals, plans, outcomes and the like. Leaders must focus heavily on discovery. What's the current state? What's the ideal state of standardization? What will it take for everyone to reach harmony by singing off the same sheet of music? There are many attributes to consider, but the key is for leaders to standardize everything that makes sense and applies.

The third step on the variation journey is measuring significance. Leaders don't know what they don't measure. Ignorance is never bliss. Did the training and organizational learning work? Has the organization succeeded in standardizing work? The only way to know is through the microscopic lens of measurement. KPIs can include variation in processes, data display, plans, operational outcomes and the like. The adage 'measure twice and cut once' applies here.

The final step of the improvement journey is for leaders to perfect outcomes. Once outcomes emerge and prove standardization reduced variation, leaders should magnify those wins. This step can take various forms. Some top performers magnify their outcomes via publications, writing books, sharing best practices and impacting the body of knowledge for the specific industry. The end goal is for leaders to share insight and knowledge internally and externally.

What's the premise of Figure 6.1 in a nutshell? As organizations learn improvement methodologies and apply them successfully, they get better over time. Part of being consistently better is standardizing the way work is done. Once the basic foundational components are in place, leaders must measure and validate outcomes to ensure the end justifies the means.

Then, organizations should perfect the art of sharing knowledge and best practices. As leaders and their organizations progress in the journey, variation declines. Thus, outcomes should improve. But, it's imperative to state again that leaders don't know what they don't measure.

Variation Risk Assessment Tools: Strategy, Operations and People

The leader then finished the Picasso, operationally speaking, with several risk assessment tools. The leader focused on strategy, operations and people. The premise was that variation posed higher levels of risk than were acceptable or healthy. But, the top leadership team had no idea of the current risk level as it was never measured.

Figure 6.2 is a risk assessment for strategy and the planning process.

Each business unit was listed in the model. Then, the leader ranked each unit on several attributes. Did the unit have a formal strategic plan? Did the unit have a knowledge plan? Did the unit have change and communications plans? Those that had formal plans were lower risk. The end goal was for all business units to have standardized formal plans for each attribute.

But the analysis revealed a different picture. Overall, as noted in Figure 6.2, 60% of the business units were high risk for strategy. This simply means they did not have adequate plans to ensure the organization was moving in the right direction. Only one of the five units was strategically prepared.

The team also learned that the organization was high risk on strategic and change plans but low risk on knowledge and communication planning. The key here was for leaders to fill the identified gaps quickly. The takeaway from Figure 6.2 is that everyone was doing something different. Variation was ramped and destroying the enterprise from the inside out.

The leader then conducted the same analysis of operations for the enterprise. The risk assessment, as noted in Figure 6.3, focused on goal attainment, improvement outcomes, data display and knowledge sharing. As noted, overall 40% of the business units were high risk in operations, 40% were low risk and only one unit was average risk.

When looking closer, the enterprise was high risk for goal attainment and data display. Simply put, the business units were all over the map with operational goal attainment. Some were high, some average and some below average. This variation equates to hundreds of millions of dollars in operational losses.

Moreover, they were all displaying data differently. Some units used run charts while others used color-coded (red, yellow, green) charts or graphs

Business Unit	Strategic Plan? 1- Formal 2- Informal 3- No Plan	Knowledge Plan? 1- Formal 2- Informal 3- No Plan	Change Plan? 1- Formal 2- Informal 3- No Plan	Communication Plan? 1- Formal 2- Informal 3- No Plan	Risk Score *Sum Columns 2-5 Lower Score = Lower Risk	Risk Level	Variation Impact
Business Unit 1	3	3	3	2	11	High Risk	High Risk Poker
Business Unit 2	1	1	1	1	4	Low Risk	Sure Bet
Business Unit 3	3	2	3	1	9	High Risk	High Risk Poker
Business Unit 4	3	1	3	1	8	Average Risk	Caution
Business Unit 5	2	3	3	2	10	High Risk	High Risk Poker

Avg Score	2.4	2.0	2.6	1.4			
Risk Level	High Risk	Low Risk	High Risk	Low Risk			

Max Risk	12
Lowest Risk	4
Avg Risk	8

Figure 6.2 Strategy Risk Assessment.

Business Unit	Organizational Goal Attainment 1->80% 2-70%-80% 3-<70%	Performance Improvement Significant Outcomes 1-Yes 2-No	Data Display 1-Run Charts 2-Color Charts 3-Variety of Displays	Knowledge Transfer 1-Formal 2-Informal 3-None	Risk Score *Sum Columns 2-5 Lower Score = Lower Risk	Risk Level	Variation Impact
Business Unit 1	3	2	3	3	11	High Risk	High Risk Poker
Business Unit 2	1	1	3	1	6	Low Risk	Sure Bet
Business Unit 3	3	2	1	2	8	Average Risk	Caution
Business Unit 4	2	1	1	2	6	Low Risk	Sure Bet
Business Unit 5	3	2	3	2	10	High Risk	High Risk Poker
Avg Score	2.4	1.6	2.2	2.0			
Risk Level	High Risk	Low Risk	High Risk	Low Risk			

Max Risk	11
Lowest Risk	4
Avg Risk	8

Figure 6.3 Operations Risk Assessment.

displaying performance over time. In contrast, some units used a combination of the two. The key here is messaging. If all the units were displaying data differently, what messages were they sending to stakeholders? The adage 'a picture is worth a thousand words' applies here. The reality was that variation in data displays conveyed conflicting and confusing signals to end users.

The leader then used the risk tool to assess people. The attributes here focused on turnover rates, culture and leadership training. The goal was to have less turnover, a culture that embraced change and leaders who were trained and proficient in improvement methodologies. The higher the risk on these attributes, the lower the organization's performance outcomes would be.

What was the current state? Let's see. As noted in Figure 6.4, 60% of the enterprise was high risk as it relates to talent management. Only 40% of the business units were low risk.

Moreover, turnover and culture were high risk on a closer look. Thus, the enterprise leaders needed to quickly focus on stopping the revolving door and improving how work gets done. The key here is that organizational resources were being dedicated to filling vacancies, and knowledge was leaving the organization at a record pace. The churn created a culture wash. Thus, quality, service and cost performance declined rapidly.

Instead of being a best practice site, the organization evolved into a master trainer and on-boarder. The reality is that competitors were reaping the benefits of the organization's investment in people. Organizational value declined as knowledge left.

The thought leader then pushed the top leadership group one step further by displaying the organization's risk in a disruption lattice. See Figures 6.5 and 6.6 for details. Figure 6.5 is the enterprise view as it relates to strategy, operations and people. This gives top leaders 'the thirty-thousand-foot view' of the enterprise's current state as a whole.

As noted in the figure, there are three zones: safe, caution and disruption. The safe zone is the place to be operationally speaking. Here, the organization is at low risk in terms of strategy, operations and people. Simply put, the organization has the plan, outcomes and talent to be an industry leader.

The caution zone is indicated as medium risk. Leaders should quickly pivot and improve organizational outcomes so disruption is avoided. In contrast, the disruption zone is the worst place to be. This zone means the enterprise is by no means equipped for success. It is essentially 'a sitting duck in an alligator-infested pond.' Practically speaking, organizations

Business Unit	Organizational Turnover 1- < 150% 2-15%-20% 3- < 20%	Culture 1- Change Acceptant 2- Neutral 3- Change Resistant	Trained Leaders in Improvement Methodology 1- Yes 2- No	Risk Score *Sum Columns 2-4 Lower Score = Lower Risk	Risk Level	Variation Impact
Business Unit 1	3	3	1	7	High Risk	High Risk Poker
Business Unit 2	3	1	1	5	Low Risk	Sure Bet
Business Unit 3	3	3	2	8	High Risk	High Risk Poker
Business Unit 4	3	1	1	5	Low Risk	Sure Bet
Business Unit 5	3	3	1	7	High Risk	High Risk Poker

Avg Score	3.0	2.2	1.2			
Risk Level	High Risk	High Risk	Low Risk			

Max Risk   8
Lowest Risk   3
Avg Risk   6

Figure 6.4   People Risk Assessment.

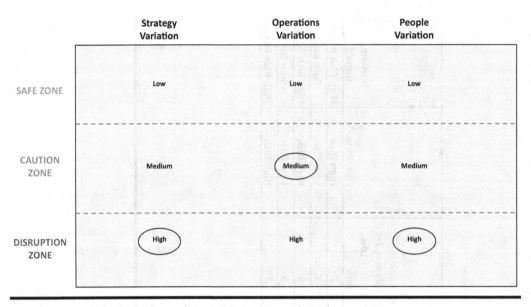

Figure 6.5 Variation Disruption Lattice: Enterprise View.

here will be disrupted sooner rather than later. It's not a matter of if, only when.

The top leaders were surprised at what was revealed in the risk model. The organization was in the disruption zone for 66% of the required attributes for success. Moreover, operations was in the caution zone. This simply means the organization as a whole was failing. The progressive operational declines were high-risk poker instead of a sure bet. The reality was simple. The organization was heading to insolvency fast, and the only course correction was an operational turnaround. Business as usual was too high risk for the journey ahead.

The thought leader's analysis concluded with Figure 6.6. This is a cross-walk view of each business unit as it relates to risk. The takeaway is 60% of the business units are in the disruption zone and at high risk of failure; 40% of the units are in the safe zone and low risk to stakeholders.

The prescription for the top leadership team was to find out what was working in unit 2 and unit 4 and then replicate their successes in the other underperforming business units. The key here is that the risk was too high, and the organization could not continue to weather the storm in its current state. The ship was sinking due to risks and its associated effects. The picture was clear: Change was on the horizon and coming faster than expected.

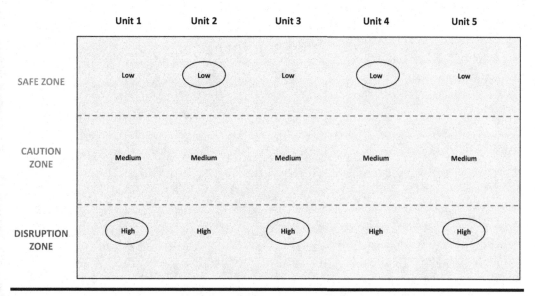

Figure 6.6   Variation Disruption Lattice: Business Unit View.

Summary

What did we learn from this case study? One, variation is a risky proposition that leaders must harness sooner rather than later. Two, variation must be controlled with standard work and improvement methodologies. Addressing variation is a process that requires a journey for the organization and its leaders. Standardization is key and takes time. Three, variation has various dimensions. To successfully crack the code, leaders must consider plans, knowledge, outcomes and culture. The goal is to standardize everything as much as possible. Variation in any of the key attributes will ultimately erode the organization from the inside out.

Finally, risk assessment tools are worth their weight in gold if leveraged properly. It is possible to leverage risk to provide insight and predict organizational impacts of variation. Leaders only know what is measured. Ignorance is never bliss. How will one know if organizational variation is high-risk poker or a sure bet if it's not measured, analyzed and displayed properly? The short answer is they won't.

Reference

1. Institute of Industrial and Systems Engineers (IISE), Lean Green Belt, 2016.

Chapter 7

Is Decision-Making a Risky Proposition?

Importance of Decisions

A decision is 'a choice that you make about something after thinking about several possibilities' (1). Decision-making is synonymous with judgement, choice, action and the like. We all make decisions daily about what to wear, what to eat, where to go, what to watch on TV and the like. Over the course of a lifetime, we make thousands (if not more) of decisions that affect us, those around us and others in the periphery whom we may never know.

For leaders, decision-making is a staple that is required to succeed in high-risk environments. As noted in Figure 7, there are a few types of decisions worth noting.

These decisions relate to strategy, operations and people. Strategic decisions are those that impact the organization's overall direction, desired end

Figure 7   Types of Decision-Making.

DOI: 10.4324/9781003335108-8   **65**

and long-term viability. These decisions may focus on the vision, mission and values statements for the enterprise as a starter. They may also include which service lines an organization will fund and execute, for example. The key here is that strategic decision-making is the thirty-thousand-foot view of leadership and critically important to many.

The next type of decisions leaders make relate to operations. These decisions are critical to the organization meeting strategic targets. Operational decisions may include budgeting, organizational training, onboarding new employees and ensuring the enterprise is compliant with regulatory requirements, for example. In layman's terms, the strategy represents the car. In contrast, operational decisions reflect the engine in the car. Without the engine, the car is essentially inoperable and will not make forward progress.

The third decision type relates to people. Whom do we hire? What knowledge and skills are needed in the organization to fulfill the mission? How will we train and impart knowledge into the talent pool to ensure the organization meets and exceeds customer requirements? What is the blueprint for the leadership succession plan to ensure depth in roles? What leadership attributes are required for top roles? Does internal talent exist to fill top leadership roles, or is external talent needed? These are just a few examples of people-related decisions. The key is that these decisions center on the organization's talent pool.

Dimensions of Decision-Making

As noted in Figure 7.1, leadership decisions have several dimensions.

For the purpose of this conversation, there are three categories. The first is urgency. Are decisions emergent, urgent or routine? The key here is the more hastily decision-making takes place, the greater is the risk involved. Emergent decisions tend to be related to crisis situations. An example would be to replace an engine in a hospital-owned ambulance that broke down while transporting a patient. This was unexpected and critical to life, health and safety of the community. Without the ambulance, emergency calls will not receive a response. Thus, humanity will suffer.

Urgent decisions are time sensitive and important but don't require an emergent response. An example would be replacing an intranet system for a large organization. This intranet is the hub for communications internally and very important to daily operations. The organization has 6 months to replace the outdated technology. The priority is escalated

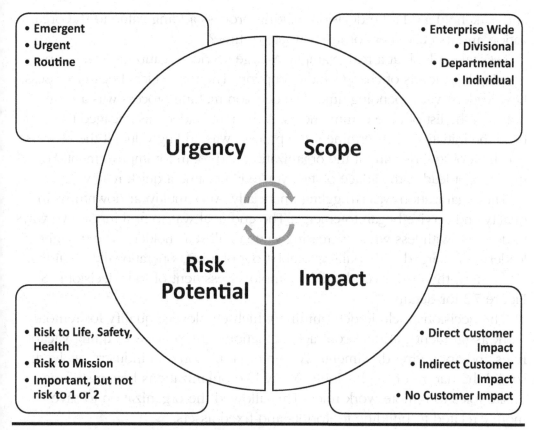

Figure 7.1   Dimensions of Decision-Making.

on the enterprise radar, but there is still adequate time to make the best decision.

Routine decisions are associated with the least risk typically. Routine decisions may include assigning new employees to a certain work area or shift. Also, routinely leaders make decisions on budgets. Do we budget dollars for extra training or stick to the basics provided in years past? There are many examples. The key here is that routine decisions are important but pose the least risk to leaders and their organizations.

Impact of Decisions

Have you ever stopped to think of the time and dollar impacts of leadership decisions? How much time do leaders spend daily, monthly or annually making decisions? What are the direct and indirect costs to the organization and stakeholders? Is the decision-making process adding value to the organization and its customers or just a waste of time?

Let's take a look at a real example. A large service organization was experiencing high levels of change and disruption. The top leaders began to assess how leaders were spending time. The decision-making process was a focal point on the list of time commitments. A thought leader was engaged to spearhead the initiative to determine if the process was adding value, if the process was high or low risk and if the organization had room for improvement. For the thought leader, the adage of 'tag, you're it' became a quick reality.

The organization was struggling financially. Also, multiyear downturns in quality and service began to emerge. The end goal was to find innovative ways to do more with less while increasing value to all stakeholders. The thought leader was charged with 'pulling a rabbit out of a hat,' operationally speaking.

To start, the leader conducted a simple assessment of four decisions. See Figure 7.2 for details.

The decisions include determining which employees qualify for remote work assignments, annual contract evaluations, the process of filling vacant roles and approving documents. As the organization and industry evolved, so did the nature of the business. Many like organizations began shifting onsite roles to remote work roles. This allowed the organization to save money related to building footprints and fixed assets.

But, the leaders had to ensure productivity stayed high and risks remained minimal. The decision to allow remote work roles was a first and impacted many thousands of employees over a large geographic area. Each decision, as noted in Figure 7.2, had ten decision points. The decision impacted 10,000 employees. Thus, leaders participated in 100,000 decisions annually for remote work assignments. This equates to over 3,000 hours of leadership time per year. The dollar amount (average) at minimum was over $300,000 in salaries per year just for this one decision alone.

The next decision point evolved around contract evaluations. Annually, organizational leaders were required to review hundreds of contracts to

Decision	Decision Points	Frequency Per Year	Total Decisions	Time (Minutes)	Time (Hours)	Average Salary Costs
Remote Work	10	10000	100000	200000	3333	$333,333.33
Contract Evaluations	12	800	9600	19200	320	$32,000.00
Refill Vacant Positions	30	1500	45000	90000	1500	$150,000.00
Approve Documents	70	365	25550	51100	852	$85,166.67
Total			180150	360300	6005	$600,500.00

Figure 7.2 Impact of Decisions.

ensure the vendors were meeting performance and regulatory requirements. Each contract evaluation had 12 decision points. This equates to almost 10,000 decisions per year requiring over 300 hours of leadership time. The dollar impact is approximately $32,000 per year in leadership salaries for this decision process alone.

The decision process to refill vacant roles had 30 decision points. The organization experienced over 1,000 vacant roles annually due to some form of turnover. These decisions to fill or not refill open roles required 1,500 hours of leadership time per year. The dollar impact was $150,000 annually in leadership salaries alone. Is turnover costly to an organization? The short answer is yes, in more ways than one.

Finally, decisions to approve documents were assessed. Each day leaders were required to approve organizational policies and the like. The process was automated but still required time commitment from leaders as they were the approvers of these documents. There were 70 decision points per day, which equates to nearly 900 hours of leadership time annually. The organization cost in leadership salary dollars was over $85,000 per year.

What's the point of the analysis? Organizational leaders had no idea of how much time they were spending each year making decisions. Moreover, no one had considered the direct costs to the organization for this activity. As I learned years ago in a microeconomics course, 'there is no such thing as a free lunch.' Translation, everything has a cost.

Practically, decisions have greater impact than most leaders realize. The greater the impact of decision-making processes, the greater is the risk. Thus, it's worth the time to understand how leaders spend their time. If four decisions cost the organization over $600,000 per year, what would the total cost be for all decision-making activities?

Decision-Making Risk Tool

The thought leader then shifted the focus of the assessment to risk. What risk did decision-making have on the organization? See Figure 7.3 for details.

As an example, the leader used the same decisions as noted in Figure 7.2. Each decision was scored on several attributes. The attributes included customer impact, scope of the organization affected by decision-making, benefit and risk potential and costs of the decision. Details are noted in Figure 7.3.

After each decision was scored, the results were surprising to the leaders: 75% of the decisions were high risk. This simply meant that each decision

Decision	Scope 1-Enterprise Wide 2-Divisional 3-Departmental	Impact 1-Directly Impacts Customer 2-Indirectly Impacts Customer 3-No Impact	Cost to Organization to Implement 1-Resources Not Budgeted or Available 2 - Resources Not Budgeted & Available 2- Resources Budgeted	Benefit Potential 1- Immediate Benefit to Life, Safety, Health 2- Immediate Benefit to Mission 3- Important, but not an immediate Benefit to 1 or 2	Nature of Decision 1- Emergent 2- Urgent 3- Routine	Risk Level 1- Risk to Life, Safety, Health 2- Risk to Mission 3- Important, but not a risk to 1 or 2	Risk Score *Sum Columns 2-7 Lower Score = Higher Risk	Risk Level
Decision 1	1	2	2	2	2	2	11	High Risk
Decision 2	1	2	3	1	3	1	11	High Risk
Decision 3	1	1	2	1	1	1	7	High Risk
Decision 4	1	2	3	2	3	2	13	Low Risk
Avg Score Risk Level	1.0 Low Risk	1.8 Low Risk	2.5 High Risk	1.5 Low Risk	2.3 High Risk	1.5 Low Risk		
Max Risk	6							
Lowest Risk	17							
Avg Risk	12							

Figure 7.3 Decision-Making Risk Assessment Tool.

had enterprise-wide impacts, imposed at least moderate costs to the organization and were a risk to life, safety, health and mission if not handled properly. The key here is each decision was like playing high-stakes poker. The right decision would provide great benefits to many. In contrast, the wrong decision would negatively jeopardize humanity.

It's also important to note that there were three high-risk attribute areas if viewing Figure 7.3 vertically. Cost to the organization for these decisions was high risk as 50% of costs imposed from the decisions were not budgeted. Also, 50% of the decisions were urgent or emergent. The key here is that as costs and time became focal points, risks to the organization and its stakeholders rose as well.

What did the leaders learn from the risk exercise? One, decisions are risky in some cases. Two, leaders must give greater attention to high-risk decisions. Three, leaders and their organizations are essentially 'driving blind' if they don't risk assess their decisions. Assuming ignorance is bliss is a risky proposition. It became abundantly clear that what the organization did not know had a great chance of harming it and its stakeholders.

Decision Matrix

Once the risk assessment was complete, the thought leader offered another tool for enterprise leaders to consider in decision-making. See Figure 7.4 for details.

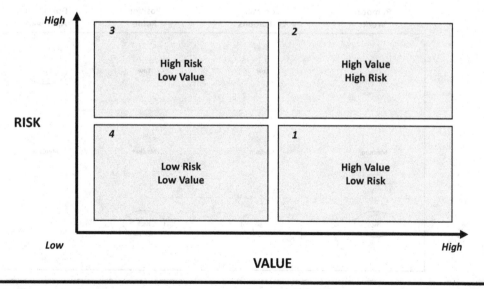

Figure 7.4 Decision Matrix.

Figure 7.4 is a simple decision matrix. Think of it as a pocket guide for leadership decision-making. This tool is a quick model to help leaders understand risk from a bird's-eye view. In short, each decision is scored as high or low as it relates to value and risk. At the end of the day, the goal is for decisions to add value and impose few risks to the organization and its stakeholders.

If a decision falls in box 1, then it is high value and low risk. This is the ideal decision for leaders to consider. If the decision qualifies for box 2, then it is high value and high risk. This is still a viable option for the enterprise, but leaders should invest more time, thought and consideration to ensure the risk is worth the reward. Box 3 denotes a decision is high risk and low value. If possible, leaders should avoid these options if at all possible. Finally, box 4 decisions provide low risk and low value. Thus, this option too is not ideal.

The takeaway is that the decision matrix can be used with any of the variables in Figure 7.3. But, leaders ultimately are charged to ensure decisions will provide the greatest value while minimizing risk when possible. If not, decision-making becomes a risky proposition.

Decision Disruption Lattice

The thought leader then provided one final tool to the top leadership cadre for consideration. Figure 7.5 is a decision disruption lattice.

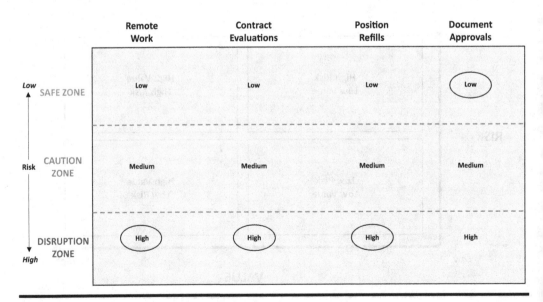

Figure 7.5 Decision Disruption Lattice.

This tool simply helps create a visual display of how risky a decision is to the organization and its stakeholders. It also provides leaders with a global view of the organization's decisions and associated risks.

As noted in Figure 7.5, there are three decision zones worth noting. The safe zone is the best place to be. Here the risk from the decisions is the lowest risk. The caution zone produces medium risk levels. Here leaders should quickly find innovative ways to pivot to the safe zone. The disruption zone is simply that, highly disruptive. If leaders find decisions are high risk as noted in Figure 7.3, they have the greatest probability of being disrupted if the decisions don't go as planned. Therefore, leaders must constantly assess, measure and pivot if risks levels continue to rise.

Let's review the four decisions addressed by the organization's leaders. Seventy-five percent of the decisions were high risk and in the disruption zone. In contrast, only 25% were in the safe zone. Not one of the decisions was medium risk to the organization and its stakeholders. The point is that there is no gray area for the leaders in this scenario. Either make good decisions that help many or bad decisions that harm the masses. There simply is no in-between. So, is decision-making a risky proposition? According to Figure 7.5, yes.

The decision to allow employees to work from home scored as high risk. Simply put, it was a risky proposition to break from the norm. Thus, it landed in the disruption zone. Keys here are for leaders to watch, assess and address immediately any issues with productivity, costs and customer satisfaction due to shifting work to a remote location. If any of these attributes are not ideal, the consequences will impact the organization as a whole and customers greatly.

Contract evaluations also landed in the disruption zone. If contract decisions are not timely, accurate and laser focused, the right vendors will not be present to ensure continuity of high-quality services. Thus, the customer and organization will be highly disrupted. Moreover, there is a high threat to life, safety, health and mission. This too is high-stakes poker.

The decision to refill vacant positions is also a risky proposition. Not filling vacancies can save a struggling organization money, but the key is to determine what impact those vacancies will have on service and quality. According to Figure 7.5, the risks associated with these decisions is very high. If leaders fail to refill critical roles, stakeholders will be at a higher risk of being harmed, if not worse. Thus, leaders should be timely and precise when making these decisions to mitigate risks.

Finally, approving documents is a low-risk, high-reward decision. Thus, leaders should engage these decisions routinely and expeditiously to ensure the most value is gained.

Summary

What did we learn with the case study on decision-making? One, decisions are important. They require a lot of leadership time and cost organizations a lot of money. Two, leadership decisions have great impact. For starters, decisions impact the organization's future direction, long-term success and operating model. Good decisions will ensure a smooth road ahead, while unsuccessful high-risk decisions will be a one-way ticket on the disruption train.

Three, decision-making has several dimensions. Leaders must prioritize decisions based on urgency, need, organizational scope, customer impact and risk. The goal is to engage choices that add the greatest amount of value and the lowest risks to all stakeholders.

Finally, leaders don't know what they don't measure. Ignorance is never bliss. As noted in Figure 7.3, all decisions pose some level of risk to the organization, leaders and other stakeholders. A simple risk tool can help organizations discern the forest for the trees.

In summary, decision-making is a risky business. Change is the new norm. As change grows, so will risk levels. Thus, leaders must be prepared to make high-risk decisions frequently in short time frames that add the greatest amount of value.

Effective leaders are those who can identify, assess, analyze and harness risk to improve humanity. If not, they will be the focal point of the next case study and a 'one-hit wonder' operationally speaking. The takeaway is to measure everything, identify risk early, leverage risk so it adds value and keep the customer at the center of all decision-making. Risky decisions can pay dividends if handled correctly or be career ending if misjudged.

Reference

1. Cambridge Dictionary. Decision. 2021. https://dictionary.cambridge.org/us/dictionary/english/decision

Chapter 8

Is Positive Leadership Reporting a Risky Proposition?

The Importance of Leadership Report-Outs

Merriam-Webster defines a report as 'A written or spoken description of a situation.' It is synonymous with providing an account of a situation or current state. One of the most common activities of leaders is reporting performance outcomes. The key is if these report-outs add value to all stakeholders or not.

There are several considerations worth noting. Are leadership report-outs important? Are they impactful? Is reporting organizational outcomes a risky business or a sure bet? Is a report-out a catalyst for change or a false sense of security? Can leaders skew the current state during report-outs to paint a positive perspective that is not reality? Is perception always reality, operationally speaking? Can leadership messaging disguise or accelerate organization failure? Are there several dimensions of leadership reporting that organizations must consider? Are leadership report-outs impactful to the organization's bottom line? Is leadership reporting a risky proposition? We answer these and other considerations in the sections that follow.

Recently, an organization's top leadership team engaged a thought leader to help with an organizational assessment. For years, the enterprise was an industry leader in the service industry. The organization was responsible for providing critical services to hundreds of thousands of customers annually over a large geographic footprint. Historically, the organization was very strong financially and was the industry best practice site in quality of services.

DOI: 10.4324/9781003335108-9

Over a several-year period, the organization's operational performance began to decline. Operational key performance indicator (KPI) goal attainment declined progressively each year by 10% or greater. Unfortunately, the impacts were significant for many customers and the organization's bottom line. Simply put, the operational downturn cost the organization tens of millions of dollars in hard dollars.

One issue arose around leadership reporting. The governing body was more than frustrated that the leadership report-outs did not mirror the organization's current state and declining trend. The organization was very bureaucratic, to say the least. It had thousands of employees and hundreds of leaders.

There were thousands of leadership meetings annually on various topics. As the organization began to decline, the leadership report-outs focused mainly on positive reporting. This method of reporting simply means the responsible leader focused solely on what was working and failed to report what was not working. The adage of 'ignorance is bliss' was the theme here. In reality, this report-out method was very dangerous. The issues were increasing over time and would not resolve themselves.

The governing body engaged the thought leader to function as the 'truth serum.' In short, they wanted a realistic picture of the organization's true performance. Also, they requested an assessment of the level of risk imposed on the organization and its stakeholders from the positive spin related to leaders positively reporting operational outcomes. The end goal was to determine if the trend would self-correct or if the governing body needed to intervene.

To start, the thought leader 'plucked' one division out of the organization's operational matrix. This division was a core function and determined if the enterprise would survive long term. Also, this function was directly tied to safety and effectiveness of services, which was the organization's 'bread and butter.'

The leader conducted a very simple analysis of leadership report-outs for the division. See Figure 8 for a summary.

As noted in the figure, the division had six layers of committees. Moreover, there were 60 committees in this division.

Committee Layers	Committees	Committee Meeting Hours Per Month	Hourly Cost Per Meeting	Cost Per Month	Cost Per Year
6	60	120	$1,500.00	$180,000.00	$2,160,000.00

Figure 8   Impact of Leadership Reporting.

Leaders attended 120 hours of meetings per month where they reported out on various KPIs, trends and other topics. Some of these meetings were regulatory requirements, while others were created by the organization. Each meeting cost the organization $1,500 per hour on average. The annual impact to the organization's bottom line was over $2 million per year. The analysis revealed nearly 100% of the leadership report-outs focused on positive reporting.

The key is that this only represents one division. Also, if the organization was failing in this critical operational component, why were leaders leveraging positive report-outs instead of painting realistic pictures of the current state so everyone could help solve the crisis? The thought leader realized early on that these positive report-out sessions were not adding value and were very expensive. The organization could not afford either of these outcomes.

Dimensions of Reporting

The leader then focused on dimensions of leadership report-outs. See Figure 8.1 for details.

There were four dimensions of interest: message, timing, impact and audience. The first dimension of effective leadership report-outs is message. There are a few thoughts to consider. Did the leadership report-outs send the right message? Messaging entails the intent of the message. Is the leader's intent to invoke an action such as to secure resourcing, support or funding to solve an issue? Is the intent to magnify underperforming outcomes to create a burning platform?

The leader realized that there was a misalignment with leadership report-outs related to messaging. Most of the leaders in the underperforming areas simply missed the mark. Whether it was intentional or not was still a mystery. Irrespectively, the message of most during report-outs was simply scanning overperforming KPIs and painting the best picture possible. There was no effort to garner support from leaders, invoke action to correct issues or create the burning platform for a turnaround.

The second dimension of leadership reporting is timing. There are several considerations here as well. Is the report-out focus aligned with the organization's current mission? Will the end justify the means? Is the report-out aligned with organizational and leadership goals? In short, will the leaders'

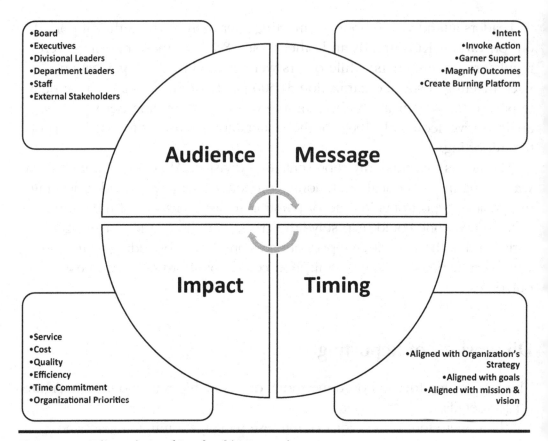

Figure 8.1   Dimensions of Leadership Reporting.

reports and subsequent actions ensure the organization's performance is in step with the current and future direction of the enterprise?

The leader realized that timing was off. Leader report-outs were positive but lacked alignment with the governing body's intent to be the quality leader in the industry. Thus, recalibration was needed. The key here is that the leadership reports felt good but were high risk to the organization and its stakeholders.

The third dimension of effective leadership reporting is impact. What impact is the leadership communication having on value? The end goal is to ensure leaders share information to the organization that helps improve the value equation. These value attributes include service, cost, quality and efficiency to start. In order for organizations to provide value to customers, leaders must align time commitments with organizational priorities.

The thought leader discovered issues here also. The leadership report-outs were not improving the value equation. Costs were too high and increasing. Similarly, service and quality continued to decline. Thus, the information being shared and the foci were off base.

The final dimension of leadership report-outs is audience. Are the right people in the room for the report-out? The intended audience may include the governing body, executives, divisional leaders, department leaders, staff and external stakeholders. The audience is dependent on the discussion topic. The key is for leaders to ensure the report-out is tailored for the audience and is impactful to create the desired response.

In retrospect, the thought leader discovered that 75% of the leadership report-out dimensions were not properly aligned. The right leaders were in the right rooms during various report-out sessions, but the message was missing the mark. Leaders failed to elevate underperforming KPIs and message the risk to the organization. Also, leadership information was out of step with the mission and desired direction of the governing body. Finally, the report-outs simply did not drive improvements in service, cost, quality or overall value. Thus, some form of correction was needed.

Long-Term Effects of Leadership Reporting

The thought leader then began to explore the long-term effects of leadership report-outs. If the information is packaged correctly and effective in evoking the right response, then value is added. It not, risk grows quickly. Figure 8.2 outlines a few impact areas of leadership reporting worth noting.

The thirty-thousand-foot view is that what leaders report or fail to report has great impact. These impacts can touch all stakeholders, ranging from

Figure 8.2   Impact of Leadership Reporting.

customers to the organization's legacy. There are short- and long-term effects of what leaders disclose or fail to mention.

In the case study, the thought leader discovered that leadership report-outs were impacting customers greatly. As quality declined, so did safety and effectiveness to many thousands of customers annually. The impact ranged from simple inconvenience to direct harm. This was high-stakes poker to say the least.

Also, effectiveness of reporting impacted the organization's brand. The organization was a long-vetted best practice site. Over several years, this brand or perception by customers declined. These declines impacted current business, future growth and all stakeholders.

One unfortunate side effect was that employee turnover spiked. Instead of being the ideal place to work, the organization evolved into a training ground. This turnover also impacted service, cost and quality unfavorably. The hard dollar effect was millions of dollars in waste over a short time period.

Finally, this situation greatly impacted leaders. Many leaders who were the positive reporters found themselves in jeopardy in the long term. They lost credibility with staff and superiors. Employee satisfaction scores plummeted. Trust also became a burning issue for the enterprise. When certain leaders reported out, it was hard for others to infer fact from fiction. The adage of 'smoke blowing' applies here.

The takeaway from Figure 8.2 is that leadership decisions and communications are greatly impactful. The information shared will impact the current state and the enterprise (and its people) for years to come. Thus, what leaders share and how that information is packaged is a high-risk proposition.

Risk Tool

The thought leader then used a simple risk tool to determine the organization's risk level. See Figure 8.3 for details.

For example, four topics were assessed to give a comparison to the governing body. The thought leader focused on report-outs related to regulatory, quality, finances and employee turnover.

Once listed, each issue is scored based on its impact to the organization, impact to the customer, legacy effect and overall risk to life, safety, health and mission. The greater the impact to the organization, its customers and its leaders, the greater the risk. The key here is that the regulatory,

Topic	Scope 1-Enterprise Wide 2-Divisional 3-Departmental	Impact 1-Directly Impacts Customer 2-Indirectly Impacts Customer 3-No Impact	Does Topic Affect the Leader's Legacy? 1- Yes 2- No	Does Topic Affect Organization's Legacy? 1- Yes 2- No	Risk Level 1- Risk to Life, Safety, Health 2- Risk to Mission 3- Important, But Not a Risk to 1 or 2	Risk Score *Sum Columns 2-6 Lower Score = Higher Risk	Risk Level	Ideal Leadership Report
Regulatory	1	1	1	1	1	5	High Risk	Realistic Report
Finances	1	1	1	1	1	5	High Risk	Realistic Report
Quality	2	1	1	1	1	6	High Risk	Realistic Report
Turnover	3	2	2	2	2	11	Average	Positive Report
Avg Score	1.8	1.3	1.3	1.3	1.3			
Risk Level	High Risk	High Risk	High Risk	High Risk	High Risk			

Max Risk	6
Lowest Risk	15
Avg Risk	11

Figure 8.3   Leadership Reporting Risk Assessment Tool.

financial and quality report-outs were high risk for the organization. Thus, realistic reporting is indicated instead of positive reporting. Realistic reporting focuses mainly on what is not working and leverages stakeholders to redirect the outcomes to a more favorable trend.

In review, the thought leaders discovered leaders had been positively reporting finances and quality even in the presence of declining outcomes. In contrast, the regulatory leaders were realistically reporting their outcomes. In short, the leaders were transparently outlining good and bad, but they always leveraged support for the bad. They were master change agents and used the report-outs to create burning platforms for corrections.

For employee turnover, this was an average risk to the organization. Thus, a mixture of positive and realistic reporting is warranted. The talent management leaders typically reported what was good but spent more time and focus on turnover hot spots. The issue was important but not out of control most of the time.

When viewing Figure 8.3 vertically, each attribute was high risk for the organization. This simply means that the macro issues plaguing the organization were high risk for impacting the enterprise as a whole, impacting legacies of all stakeholders and a risk to life, safety, health and mission. Thus, positive reporting alone is a risky proposition for the enterprise and its governing body.

The thought leader packaged the findings and shared this insight with the governing board. The top leaders were somewhat surprised on one hand. But, what others expected was validated. As a result, an organizational turnaround ensued. The change was warranted.

The organization was restructured and shifted its focus away from positive report-outs to ones focused on realistic operational assessments. Unfortunately, the risk assessment was needed years earlier. The adage of 'a day late and a dollar short' applies here. Irrespectively, the governing body's assumptions were validated by the risk portrait and justified an intervention.

The reality was simple. For one reason or another, the wool was pulled over the governing body's eyes for several years. The organizational declines were real and overlooked. Positive spins on outcomes reporting felt good at the moment but were costly in many ways to many stakeholders for years to come. The end simply did not justify the means, unfortunately.

Summary

What did we learn from the case study? One, leaders don't know what they don't measure. Seventy-five percent of the leadership report-out dimensions were not aligned with the organization's mission or desired future direction, but no one ever took the time to measure. The organizational leaders were simply high risk for the report-outs. The information being shared was more feel-good than geared toward transforming the organization's outcomes. The adage of 'politically correct, but not effective' applies here.

Two, leadership information sharing and report-outs are very impactful. What is reported or not reported can grossly affect all stakeholders ranging from customers to the organization's legacy. Moreover, these impacts have significant long-term consequences. Change is the new norm. As change grows, so does risk. How leaders package and deliver information will determine if the organization thrives, survives or fails long term in high-risk environments.

Finally, the organization as a whole was failing for various reasons. At the core was risk that was existing under the leadership radar. The governing body was ill informed. The leadership report-outs were grossly positive reports that were not what the leadership cadre needed to hear.

The lesson learned is that risk is a reality and highly impactful. Leaders must be courageous and willing to share the bad with the good. Ignorance is never bliss. Effective leaders are those who can package, message and leverage the current state to paint an impactful picture to drive significant outcomes. Otherwise, positive reporting will be a risky proposition that will erode the organization from the inside out.

Chapter 9

Leveraging Risk to Grow Organizational Hierarchy: Is It Value Added or a Waste of Resources?

The Importance of Hierarchy

What is an organizational hierarchy? The term 'corporate hierarchy' refers to the arrangement and organization of individuals within a corporation according to power, status and job function. In general, a hierarchy is any system or organization in which people or groups are ranked one above the other according to status or authority' (1). In layman's terms, leaders often use hierarchy in reference to reporting structures or organizational levels. The terminology varies based on industry and organization type.

Generally, there are several considerations to how organizations structure their businesses. Hierarchy in some instances is synonymous with bureaucracy. The bureaucratic undertone is that heavily structured organizations tend to be slow and less agile and require a lot more work to provide goods or services as compared to their leaner counterparts. Is this perception always reality? The short answer is not always. But, it's important to note that more processes, steps and levels needed to complete tasks or work can lead to excessive financial overhead and less value to the customer base if not handled correctly.

DOI: 10.4324/9781003335108-10

Let's take a closer look at a real example. A large service organization began its journey to higher-level performance. The end goal was to be the industry and market leader in its particular field. The measures of success were service, cost, quality and efficiency. The first step of the enterprise was leadership changes across the board.

A new top leader was introduced to the organization. The agenda was simple. The organization needed to reduce costs, improve quality of services and be the most efficient provider of services in the market space. The first directive was an organizational restructure.

The new leader gave a directive to all subordinates to reduce the hierarchy to five levels from the top leader. This sent shock waves through the organization. These changes would fundamentally change the way the organization would run, perform and function. This was definitely a change from the norm. Some changes came with attrition, turnover and the like. In contrast, some organizational flattening came through forced displacements.

Irrespective of the method, the organization became leaner, more horizontal in structure and more agile quickly. The hierarchical compression saved hard dollars, but many leaders were hard pressed to find other benefits. It begs the question, are radical organizational structural changes always ideal? In reality, sometimes speed to execution is good, while other times it may not last or achieve the desired end in the long term.

Within a couple years of the initial restructure, the organization began to grow its structure again both vertically and horizontally. The enterprise experienced waves of growth followed by waves of cutting. The cyclical pattern was repetitive and continued for some time. The need for more discipline was evident. Leaders began to ask, 'Why do we continue to find ourselves in this situation over and over again?'

To compound the issue, the organization began to see operational declines. These downturns impacted the organization's bread and butter: service, cost, quality and efficiency. The organization experienced several years of lessening key performance indicator (KPI) goal attainment for these attributes. The declines equated to hundreds of millions of dollars in hard dollar losses. Moreover, hundreds of thousands of customers were impacted unfavorably over a very large geographic region.

This leads us to several considerations. Is adding leadership roles a risky proposition? Is hierarchy growth multidimensional or unifocal? Is it possible to risk assess leadership decisions to grow the organization's hierarchy? Can adding too many organizational layers sink the operational ship, or is it always smooth sailing? How may leadership roles and levels are too much? Is more always better in terms of top roles?

In the following sections, we answer these considerations and more.

Dimensions of Hierarchy Growth

When leaders and their organizations contemplate growing the organizational structure, there are several dimensions to consider. See Figure 9 for details.

First, leaders should focus on need. Is there a need for the role(s)? The need often spawns from regulatory requirements or other operational aspects. For example, if the organization adds a service line and needs a leader with a specific skill set to run that service, then it may be justifiable to add the role.

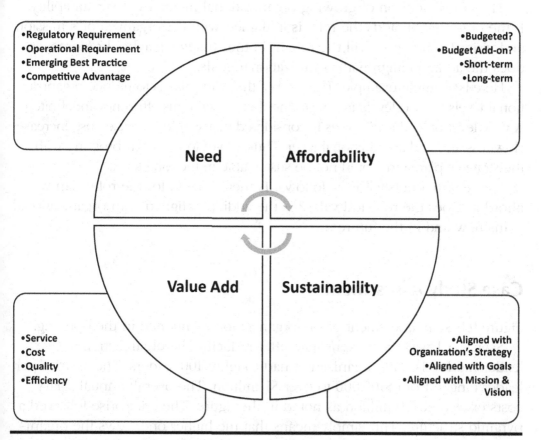

Figure 9   Dimensions of Organizational Hierarchy Growth.

Need for the role(s) may also emerge from industry best practices to have certain roles, skill sets and the like. Without them, competitors may be better positioned to take or sustain market share. Irrespective of the need, leaders must answer, 'Does the organization need this role?' If the answer is yes, then proceed to the next dimension. If no, don't add the role.

The second dimension of growing organizational structures is affordability. This correlates to available resources. The question here is, 'Can we afford to add the role?' Affordability has three perspectives: now, short run and long term. Can the organization afford to fund the role now, in the near future and long term? If the answer is yes, proceed to the next dimension. If no, then strong caution and consideration are warranted.

The third dimension relates to value. Does the role addition add value? Value can take many forms. To start, does the role's presence improve service, cost or quality? Will the role add or detract from efficiency? If the role adds value, then proceed to the next dimension. If value is lost, further consideration is warranted.

The last dimension of growing organizational hierarchy is sustainability. If the organization adds the role, is it aligned with the organization's mission and vision? Long term, will the role fit in the strategic playbook? Moreover, does the addition align with organizational goals?

Here is a simple example. The goal of the enterprise is to reduce organizational levels by two levels in a year and then sustain this efficiency indefinitely. A new level of leadership roles is considered that would increase cost, increase slowness and add an additional layer. Thus, it would not align properly with the strategic plan and would not be sustainable in the long term.

Figure 9 in a nutshell is as follows. Is there a need for the role? Can we afford it? Does the role add value? Is the addition aligned with organizational plans now and in the future?

Case Study Assessment

Figure 9.1 is an assessment of the organization mentioned in the opening.

Scenario 1 was the current state after reducing the organization to five leadership levels. The organization had roughly 100 leaders. The salaries per leader ranged from $100,000 to over $1 million. The overall annual salary costs exceeded $20 million as noted in the figure. The enterprise followed a pyramid structure. This simply means that the higher one views the organizational chart, the fewer positions exist.

Scenario 1

Level	Salary	Count	Total Salary $
5	$1,500,000.00	1	$1,950,000.00
4	$500,000.00	8	$5,200,000.00
3	$300,000.00	5	$1,950,000.00
2	$200,000.00	15	$3,900,000.00
1	$100,000.00	70	$9,100,000.00
5		99	$22,100,000.00

Scenario 2

Level	Salary	Count	Total Salary $
7	$1,500,000.00	1	$1,950,000.00
6	$1,000,000.00	1	$1,300,000.00
5	$750,000.00	4	$3,900,000.00
4	$500,000.00	12	$7,800,000.00
3	$300,000.00	24	$9,360,000.00
2	$200,000.00	24	$6,240,000.00
1	$100,000.00	70	$9,100,000.00
7		136	$39,650,000.00

Summary

Cost Increase ($)	$17,550,000.00
Cost Increase (%)	79.41%
Level Increase (#)	2
Level Increase (%)	40%
Leader Count Increase (#)	37
Leader Count Increase (%)	37%
Reporting Ratio (Level 3 to Level 2)	200%
Reporting Ratio (Level 2 to Level 1)	60%

Figure 9.1 Organizational Hieararchy Growth Assessment.

As time passed, the organization relaxed and began to bloat once again. The top leadership team added nearly 40 positions over a short time period as noted in scenario 2. This represented the future state that evolved into the new state. In short, the additional roles increased annual salaries by almost $18 million per year. The biggest add-ons related to divisional-level roles.

It's important to note that the organizational downturn began when the hierarchy growth occurred. The enterprise not only added almost 40 roles, but it also added two new levels of leadership. This addition in levels increased the bureaucracy by 40% from that perspective.

Moreover, the salary costs increased by almost 80%. The total number of leadership roles increased by 37%. We can't forget that the value KPIs goal attainment also declined by roughly 30% during this time. Was more leadership better? Not in this case.

As noted, the biggest increases were divisional leaders. When comparing the ratio of leaders in level 3 to level 2, the ratio increased by 200% in scenario 2. When comparing level 2 to level 1 leaders, this ratio increased by 60%. What does this mean practically?

The organization historically adopted the pyramid structure. Higher levels on the organizational chart had fewer leaders. The model diverted away from a pyramid structure to a box as it relates to divisional leaders. There was a 1:1 ratio between leader level 2 and level 3 roles as noted in the figure. Thus, the middle section of the hierarchy was overextended and bloated.

Another interesting point worth noting relates to the return on this salary investment. For every dollar spent on new roles, the organization lost nearly $17 operationally. Was this a risky proposition? By all accounts, yes.

Risk Assessment Tool

In retrospect, the organization used a risk tool to risk assess several roles that were added. See Figure 9.2 for details.

Is looking back ideal? It is, for learning what not to repeat. But, it's not ideal for solving a multimillion-dollar loss that already happened. The adage 'a day late, a dollar short' applies here.

In Figure 9.2, the roles were listed in the first column. Then, each role was assessed on four attributes: need, affordability, impact on bureaucracy and benefit potential. Simply put, did the organization need the role? Was the role affordable based on current resources levels? Did the role's introduction into the operational canvas add to or decrease bureaucracy? Finally, did the role add any benefit to life, safety, health or mission?

As noted in the figure, ten sample roles were chosen from the subgroup of those added. Eighty percent of the roles were high risk. This means leaders should not have added the roles based on the organization's current state. Only 20% of the roles were average risk. Thus, leaders would need to proceed with caution in growing the organization's structure with these additions.

When viewing Figure 9.2 vertically for each attribute, the results are interesting. Only 20% of the added roles were required by regulations or

Role	Role Need? 1-Not Required 2-Required	Can the Organization Afford the Role? 1-No 2-Yes	Impact on Organization's Bureaucracy 1- Adds 2 -Neutral 3- Decreases	Benefit Potential 3- Immediate Benefit to Life, Safety, Health 2- Immediate Benefit to Mission 1- Important, but not an immediate Benefit to 1 or 2	Risk Score *Sum Columns 2-5 Lower Score = Higher Risk	Risk Level	Growth Decision
Role 1	1	1	1	1	4	High Risk	Don't Add
Role 2	1	1	1	1	4	High Risk	Don't Add
Role 3	1	1	1	1	4	High Risk	Don't Add
Role 4	1	1	1	1	4	High Risk	Don't Add
Role 5	1	1	1	1	4	High Risk	Don't Add
Role 6	1	2	2	1	6	High Risk	Don't Add
Role 7	2	2	2	1	7	Average	Caution
Role 8	2	2	2	1	7	Average	Caution
Role 9	1	2	2	1	6	High Risk	Don't Add
Role 10	1	2	1	1	5	High Risk	Don't Add

Figure 9.2   Risk Assessment Tool: Organizational Hierarchy Growth.

operations. The organization could only afford to add 50% of the roles listed in the subgroup. Sixty percent of the roles added bureaucracy or slowness to the organization. Finally, none of the roles added an immediate benefit to life, safety, health or mission. They were important but not critical to the operation.

What are the key points from Figure 9.2? One, expanding the organization's hierarchy was high risk from many angles. Most of the added roles were 'nice-to-haves' or 'like-to-haves' instead of 'complete value added.' Two, 80% of the roles should never have been added from this subgroup. The risks were way too high, and failure was all but certain.

Three, the enterprise had no idea these decisions and bloating would be so risky. Leaders don't know what they don't measure. Each change evokes some level of risk. The greater the change, the greater is the risk. As learned in the case study, what leaders don't know can and will eventually hurt them, the organization and its customers.

Decision Matrix

To avoid the pitfalls in the case study, let's look at a simple decision matrix. See Figure 9.3 for details.

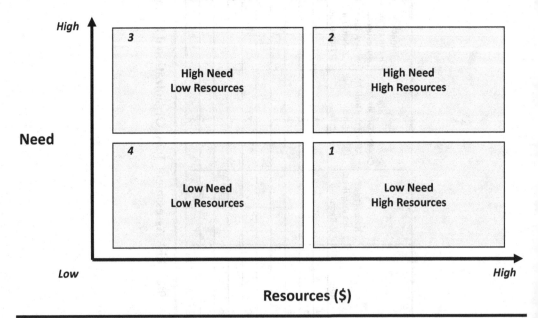

Figure 9.3   Organizational Hierarchy Growth Decision Matrix.

At a glance, leaders should place each role addition decision into a matrix. Obviously, there are more considerations than listed in Figure 9.3. During the busyness of leadership, generally speaking, this tool will tell leaders when to run for the hills or grow the hierarchy.

Here, two attributes are listed: need and resourcing. The same theme follows. Can the organization afford the role? Is there a justifiable need for the role addition? As noted in box 2, when need is high and resources are plentiful, leaders should proceed with the addition consideration. When resources and need for the role are low, as noted in box 4, this is a no-go zone. This simply means risks are too high to add the role. When there is a high need and low resources (box 3), leaders must proceed with caution before growing the hierarchy.

Finally, as noted in box 1, when the need is low and resources are high, leaders should also proceed with caution. The key here is to risk assess the roles as noted in Figure 9.2 and consider the dimensions in Figure 9. The end goal is to add roles only if they add value in some form, are needed and align with organizational plans. Otherwise, risks are too high, and it becomes spending for the sake of spending instead of a good investment.

Summary

The case study provides great insight into risk and its potential on organizational hierarchies. We learned that adding leadership roles is a risky proposition. Although leadership role growth seems ideal from afar, the clarity provided by risk assessments may often unveil a mirage instead of an ideal oasis. Thus, perception is not always reality.

The new normal is change and the only constant in today's world. As change grows, so will risk. The key is measurement. Leaders don't know what they don't measure. Moreover, what they don't know can and will eventually hurt them in the long run. Hierarchy growth is a multidimensional concept that requires significant consideration. The end goal is to ensure the organization's structure adds value instead of sinking the ship.

Effective leaders are those who make decisions to grow the organization's hierarchy with insight, risk awareness and caution. What sparkles does not always shine. As noted in the case study, for each dollar invested in leadership role additions, there was a $17 operational loss. Thus, growing the hierarchy was a waste of resources instead of a value added.

In summary, more is not always better. Leaders and their organizations have to right-size their operating footprints based on need, resourcing, strategic alignment and sustainability. It's better to choose wisely than to jump the fence for the greener grass that does not exist. The key is measuring, assessing and leveraging risk to grow the organization's hierarchy wisely instead of recklessly.

Reference

1. Investopedia Business Essentials. Corporate hierarchy. 2021. https://www.investopedia.com/terms/c/corporate-hierarchy.asp

Risk Assessing Succession Planning: Is the Talent Pipeline Full or All Dried Up?

Importance of Depth in Roles

One of the hottest topics in thought leadership circles is knowledge transfer. This concept is synonymous with knowledge sharing, organizational knowledge, talent management and the like. By definition, knowledge transfer is 'the practical problem of transferring knowledge from one part of the organization to another' (1). In reality, knowledge transfer has many components.

As we learned over the years, sharing knowledge goes beyond just a person-to-person transfer. It entails transferring knowledge from one person to another, across departments or divisions, across the enterprise as a whole and even externally. Internal knowledge transfer tends to focus on ensuring the organization has the talent it needs to meet and exceed customer requirements. People need knowledge, skills, training and the like to complete work. Thus, organizational knowledge is complex and multidimensional.

External knowledge transfer refers to how the organization shares knowledge outside the organization. This sharing can be with partners, peers, potential partners, the industry as a whole and even other industries. Knowledge shared outside the organization typically takes the form of published articles, written books and presentations by leaders and employees on current topics relevant to the industry and/or the market as a whole. The key here is to share best practices and insight so others can be better tomorrow than they were yesterday.

One often overlooked aspect of knowledge transfer is succession planning. Succession planning is 'a focused process for keeping talent in the pipeline' (2). This concept is synonymous with depth in roles, planning talent needs for tomorrow and crisis planning in hopes of avoiding a crisis. The key is that succession planning is crucial to long-term organizational success. Without the proper knowledge levels and people, organizations will become obsolete quickly.

Is succession planning a top organizational priority? Is planning for the talent pipeline a risky proposition or a sure bet? Can a simple risk assessment tool help organizational leaders avoid a talent crisis? Does succession planning apply only to leadership?

Should leaders ensure depth in roles exists in other critical roles outside of leadership? Can leaders successfully plan for the future to ensure the right knowledge is present without measuring and analyzing the current state? Is a lack of succession planning costly to organizations and a risk to its financial future?

We answer these and other considerations in the sections that follow.

Dimension of Succession Planning

There are four dimensions succession planners must consider. See Figure 10 for details.

The first dimension is the current talent pool. Thought leaders must answer several key questions.

Is the talent pipeline full or empty? Are there any hard to fill roles? If so, what are they and where are they located? Does the organization have a cross-training program to share knowledge across business units and roles? Is turnover in or out of control? Are there any high vacancy rate areas? If so, where are they? Also, is the role vacancy issue recurrent or a one-time issue? How does the organization share knowledge currently?

The key with the talent pool is a current state assessment. Where is the talent? Where are the gaps? Are fundamental processes and structures in place to ensure talent is available for the organization to fulfill its mission now and in the future? What hot spots exist that need an emergency response?

The second dimension of succession planning is organizational knowledge. This concept can take many forms, including but not limited to values, norms, documented processes, plans and the like. The key here is to discern

Figure 10   Dimensions of Succession Planning.

how the organization works. The end goal is to ensure the organization's work processes are captured in some form.

This knowledge should be housed in a knowledge management system. Moreover, it should be documented, standardized, available when needed and current. At the end of the day, regardless of who is or is not in the organization, work continues. Documented knowledge will ensure continuity of services so work is not interrupted.

The third dimension of success planning is risk. Merriam-Webster defines risk as 'the possibility of loss or injury' (3). In talent management, leaders must consider how risky certain attributes are to the organization and its customers. These risks may include unique roles, critical roles, shortages of roles and market competition for talent. In short, there are a few considerations to keep this concept very simple.

Are there any unique roles that are high risk if they become vacant? Is the market demand and supply of various roles in balance or are shortages present? Are competitors drafting the organization's talent away? If risk exists, leaders must address it promptly. Otherwise, the organization will be a day late and a dollar short from a talent perspective.

Here is a simple example. Recently, a news report came across a local TV station. A new mayor was elected and realized there were issues with a city department. The department recently lost a seasoned, long-tenure leader to retirement. A direct report leader in the department was appointed to the department head role. The problem was this new leader lacked experience, knowledge and insight to adequately run the department.

An independent audit team was hired to assess the department's performance. The audit revealed gross mismanagement for a period of time. As a result, the leader was terminated. Also, outside consultants were hired to restructure the department and solve significant issues.

The outside consulting help and years of mismanagement cost the city millions of dollars to correct. One notable quote from the mayor was, 'When the long-term leader left, they took all the knowledge with them as to how to run the department.' The local government had no knowledge transfer plan, and the knowledge left with the seasoned leader. Thus, missteps occurred, and a crisis ensued. Is succession planning a risky proposition? The short answer is yes.

The last dimension of succession planning is the knowledge plan. An organizational knowledge plan is multidimensional. For this conversation, let's keep it simple. Thought leaders need a knowledge plan that is, most importantly, aligned with the enterprise strategic plan. This includes a cyclical process wherein talent is assessed, gaps are identified and solutions follow to fill the gaps.

It's imperative to ensure a budget exists so the talent pipeline is full. There are several considerations worth noting. Is funding available to pay at or above market salary rates for all roles? Is funding in the budget for performance bonuses? Are pensions fully funded?

How much will organizational training cost annually? What training is needed and required? What goals for basic training, upskilling and retention are in the strategic plan? The key is to measure the current state, identify opportunities and set goals to fill the gaps.

Finally, the knowledge plan should include a knowledge system. This system houses all the organization's documented knowledge. There are several key points to remember here. The documented knowledge may take the form of policies, procedures, quick guides and the like. This knowledge must be standardized, current, reviewed often and readily available to end users at a moment's notice.

Risk Tools

As change increases, so will risk. Thus, leaders must risk assess their succession plans and various corresponding attributes. Otherwise, ignorance will be bliss, and risk will disrupt the organization. Let's take a closer look at a real example.

A large service organization began its knowledge transfer journey. The catalyst for the journey was the COVID-19 pandemic. For years, the organization funded several unique roles. One in particular related to emergency management. The organization only had one role for a large enterprise. Leaders often failed to appreciate or see the value in this role.

For years, emergency management was a mundane function that received very little attention. The emergency manager only interacted with enterprise leaders during drills, tabletop exercises and the like. The focal points were checking the boxes for certain regulatory requirements. The perception by many leaders was this role was a formality and low risk as emergencies almost never occurred.

At one point, organizational leaders discussed cutting the role for cost savings purposes. The adage of 'cut off your nose to spite your face' applied here unknowingly. Shortly after, the pandemic arrived. The world was thrust into a crisis, and emergency management became front and center. This role's prominence, exposure and influence skyrocketed as command centers began running certain industries. The organization in context was run by its emergency command center for well over a year while the pandemic surged.

As the situation evolved, the enterprise leaders began to focus on succession planning for this unique role and others. See Figure 10.1 for details.

In short, ten roles were identified as high priorities as noted in the figure. Each role was risk assessed on several attributes. Did the role have an enterprise, divisional or departmental impact? Was demand for the role high in the market? Was market supply of the role low or high? Did the role directly impact the customer? The greater the demand for the role and the greater the direct impact to customers equated to higher risk for the organization.

As noted, 80% of the unique roles were high risk. Only two roles in the sample were average or low risk. When viewing Figure 10.1 vertically, high-risk attributes for the enterprise were the impact on the customer, market demand and market supply. The key here was that the organization's talent pipeline was high risk. Simply put, the organization was at high risk to be disrupted if these roles became vacant. Lack of succession planning ensured

Role View

Role	Role Scope 1-Enterprise Wide 2-Divisional 3-Departmental	Impact 1-Directly Impacts Customer 2-Indirectly Impacts Customer 3-No Impact	Market Demand for the Role 1-High 2-Medium 3-Low	Market Supply for the Role 1-Low 2-Medium 3-High	Risk Level 1-Risk to Life, Safety, Health 2-Risk to Mission 3-Important, but not a risk to 1 or 2	Risk Score *Sum Columns 2-6 Lower Score = Higher Risk	Risk Level
Role 1	3	1	1	1	1	7	High Risk
Role 2	3	1	1	1	1	7	High Risk
Role 3	3	1	1	1	1	7	High Risk
Role 4	3	2	2	2	2	11	Low Risk
Role 5	2	2	2	1	2	9	High Risk
Role 6	2	2	2	1	2	9	High Risk
Role 7	2	1	2	1	3	9	High Risk
Role 8	1	1	1	1	3	7	High Risk
Role 9	1	1	1	2	3	8	High Risk
Role 10	1	2	2	2	3	10	Average
Avg Score	2.1	1.4	1.5	1.3	2.1		
Risk Level	Low Risk	High Risk	High Risk	High Risk	Low Risk		

Figure 10.1 Risk Assessment Tool: Organizational Succession Planning.

the organization and its customers would be greatly impacted if depth for each role was not quickly identified.

The organization then grew the assessment for succession planning to focus on its major business units. See Figure 10.2 for details.

Five business units were selected for the assessment. Each unit was also scored on various attributes. What percentage of roles in each unit had a primary and backup person? Did the organization have paired work assignments and a cross-training program? What percentage of the critical roles were identified? The premise was simple: Where is the risk, and is it being mitigated properly?

As noted in the figure, 60% of the business units were high risk. The leaders had not properly identified critical roles and implemented knowledge sharing to ensure there was adequate depth in those roles. Only 40% of the units were low risk as it relates to succession planning.

All the attributes, when viewing the tool vertically were high risk. The key here is the organization was unprepared in terms of talent management. The leaders simply did not know what they didn't know. The business units needed to quickly invest resources in identifying critical roles and training and filling the talent pipeline. Overall, knowledge transfer was just a fancy tagline instead of an operational reality.

The organization needed a formal succession planning process and structure tied back to the knowledge plan. If not corrected quickly, rough waters were ahead. Was the talent pipeline full or all dried up? In short, the latter was definitely the case here.

Entity View

Entity View	% of Roles with Primary + Backup Person? 1- <70% 2-70%-80% 3- >80%	Does the Organization Have Paired Assignments Program? 1-No 2-Yes	Does the Organization Have Cross Training Program? 1-No 2-Yes	% of Critical Roles Identified? 1- <70% 2-70%-80% 3- >80%	Risk Level 1- Risk to Life, Safety, Health 2- Risk to Mission 3- Important, but not a risk to 1 or 2	Risk Score *Sum Columns 2-6 Lower Score = Higher Risk	Risk Level
Entity 1	1	1	1	1	1	5	High Risk
Entity 2	1	1	1	1	1	5	High Risk
Entity 3	2	1	1	1	1	6	High Risk
Entity 4	3	2	2	2	2	11	Low Risk
Entity 5	3	2	2	2	3	12	Low Risk

Avg Score	2.0	1.4	1.4	1.4	1.6
Risk Level	High Risk	High Risk	High Risk	High Risk	High Risk

Max Risk	5
Lowest Risk	13
Avg Risk	9

Figure 10.2   Risk Assessment Tool: Organizational Succession Planning.

Summary

What did we learn from the case study? One, succession planning is and should be a top organizational priority. The key is to ensure leaders are proactive in planning for current and future talent needs. Far too often, organizations don't realize a crisis is brewing until is too late. Subsequently, this reactive approach has disastrous effects on the organization's brand, finances and quality of services.

Two, planning for the talent pipeline is a risky proposition. As we learned, talent management is not a sure bet. This concept is multidimensional, and each dimension can fill the pipeline or drain it if not addressed properly. Leaders simply don't know what they don't measure. Simple risk tools can help organizations and their leaders avoid a talent crisis if leveraged properly.

Three, succession planning is not exclusive to leadership roles. This is a common misperception and pitfall of many organizations. In succession planning, leaders must see the forest for the trees. Missing a critical role such as the emergency manager in the previous example is a land mine waiting to explode. Thus, risk matters in many venues and at various levels.

In summary, risk and knowledge matter. The end goal is to maximize organizational knowledge and minimize risk. The key is understanding the current talent pool, formally documenting the organization's knowledge, identifying and mitigating risks and crafting a well-thought-out knowledge plan. Knowledge is the greatest resource to any organization. Effective leaders are those who can leverage knowledge and harness risk to ensure the talent pipeline is full instead of bone dry.

References

1. Wikipedia. Knowledge transfer. 2021. https://en.wikipedia.org/wiki/Knowledge_transfer
2. Society for Human Resource Management (SHRM). *Engaging in Succession Planning.* www.shrm.org/resourcesandtools/tools-and-samples/toolkits/pages/engaginginsuccessionplanning.aspx
3. Merriam-Webster. 2022. https://www.merriam-webster.com/dictionary/risk

Chapter 11

Risk Assessing Leadership Credentials: Is It a Game Changer or Just Another Plaque on the Wall?

Importance of Credentials

Is a credential the key that unlocks doors to new opportunities? Are all credentials a game changer for the leader or just another plaque on the wall? Will credentials ensure leaders make more money and receive more promotions with time? Is a credential a sure bet or a gamble? Will a leadership credential add credibility? Is the extra time, cost and investment worth pursuing credentials beyond the basics required for a role? Will a credential provide a competitive advantage for leaders via promotions and performance incentives and with competitors? We answer these and more considerations in the sections that follow.

A *credential* is 'a piece of any document that details a qualification, competence, or authority issued to an individual by a third party with a relevant or *de facto* authority or assumed competence to do so' (1). In layman's terms, credentials are synonymous with credibility, role requirements, expertise, knowledge and the like. The key is that credentials vary among roles, industries and the market in general. But credentials in many respects matter, add value if leveraged properly and are worth the consideration.

DOI: 10.4324/9781003335108-12

Recently, a large service organization was reviewing its knowledge plan for hundreds of leaders. This was part of the annual strategic planning process. The goal was to ensure leaders possessed the basic credentials for their specific roles and to identify credentials that would improve organizational performance, improve its market footprint and reward top performers with growth opportunities.

During the review, the team focused on four dimensions of leadership credentials. See Figure 11 for details.

Figure 11 outlines four basic considerations for leadership credential investment. First, several aspects of costs are considered. What are the direct costs of the credential? What are the indirect costs or opportunity costs for the investment? An opportunity cost is the next best thing that could have been done with those dollars invested in the credential. A formal definition of *opportunity cost* is, 'the forgone benefit that would have been derived by an option not chosen' (2). Are there initial

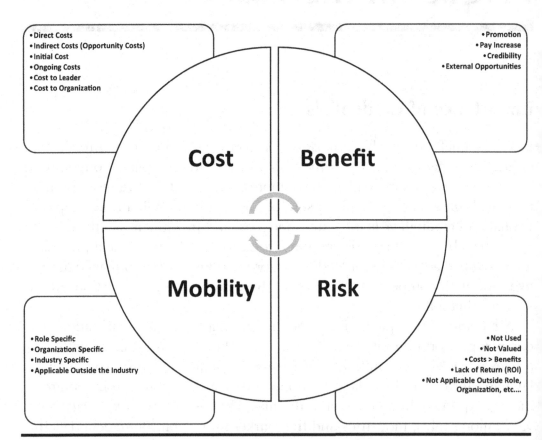

Figure 11   **Dimensions of Leadership Credentials.**

and ongoing costs for the credential? What is the cost to the leader and organization?

The second dimension in leadership credential investments is benefit. Simply put, what is the expected gain from earning the credential to the leader, organization, industry and customer base? Also, will the credential provide promotion opportunities and pay increases? Will the credential add credibility to the leader's brand and afford external opportunities such as consulting, teaching or knowledge sharing? The end goal is to ensure the benefits outweigh the risks.

The third dimension is risk. There are several considerations for both leaders and organizations. What is the risk if the credential is earned but not used? What's the probability that the credential will not be valued by the organization, peers, industry, and so forth? Will the costs of the investment exceed the overall benefit? Is the credential limited in terms of portability?

The final dimension relates to mobility. Is the credential role- or organization-specific? Is it industry specific? Can the leader use the credential outside of the industry? The key here is to determine the reach of the credential. Generally speaking, the greater the reach, the greater the value.

Case Study

Once the four dimensions were defined, the team pulled a sample of leaders to review their credentials and outcomes once achieved. The goal was to estimate the return on specific credentials and outline the low-risk, high-reward investments. Were the investments a game changer for the leaders or just another plaque on the wall? Let's see.

Leader 1 was a divisional leader in a large business unit. The leader had significant responsibility, and the unit impacted thousands of customers annually. The leader earned a bachelor's degree and a master's degree. Both degrees were portable to other industries. Later, the leader invested in a Six Sigma Black Belt to increase performance improvement capabilities. Finally, the leader earned a doctorate that was industry-specific.

It's imperative to note that only the bachelor's and master's degrees were required for the role. All other credentials were above and beyond role requirements. The total investment was over $250,000 in direct costs for the base credentials.

Leader 2 was a department-level leader. This leader too invested in bachelor's and master's degrees that were industry-specific and role-required. Later, the leader followed a similar path and earned a doctorate that was portable outside the industry. As part of this credential, the leader earned a Six Sigma Black Belt to round out the skill set. The overall direct investment was $200,000.

Leader 3 was an enterprise leader for the service company. This leader earned a bachelor's degree and later a master's degree. Both degrees were industry-specific and role-required. The leader also invested in another leadership certification that was industry specific but optional. Thus, it was not recognized or valued in other industries. The direct cost of the specialty certification was $15,000 initially with ongoing costs annually related to continuing education.

Were these high-risk propositions or a sure bet? The organization used a simple risk assessment tool to objectively score each credential. Overall, as noted in Figure 11.1, the lower the score, the greater the risk.

As noted, each credential was scored on several factors. Was the credential role or industry specific, or was it applicable in other fields? Was the credential required for the current role? Was the credential required for the next-level role? Did the credential guarantee a pay increase or promotion?

In retrospect, the organization learned that bachelor's degrees, master's degrees and technical certifications for specific roles were low risk. Thus, they were a safe bet and a good investment. In contrast, the risk tool showed that the Six Sigma Black Belt credential was average risk.

Therefore, the organization should proceed with caution when investing in these credentials. Practically, this credential has both risks and significant benefits. The key is to ensure those who will use the credential successfully and have the greatest benefit potential for a return would receive the investment. Otherwise, it is training for the sake of training and a waste of resources.

The risk tool also revealed that the doctorate degree and leadership certification were high risk. Thus, the organization should postpone this investment and focus on the other lower-risk credentials. The high-risk credentials were limited in portability and overall value to the organization's mission. Simply put, they were a 'nice-to-have' and not a 'have-to-have.'

Let's look back at the three leaders previously noted. Leader 1 invested $250,000 in credentials. Most of them were not role-required. Only 50% of the credentials were low risk. The Black Belt and doctorate degree were average or above risk. Post credentials, the leader received several

Credential	Is Credential Portable? 1- Role Specific 2- Industry Specific 3- Applicable Outside Industry	Required for Current Role? 1-No 2-Yes	Required for Desired Next Level Role? 1-No 2-Yes	Guarantee Promotion? 1- No 2-Yes	Guarantee Pay Increase? 1- No 2- Yes	Risk Score *Sum Columns 2-6 Lower Score = Higher Risk	Risk Level	Decision Point
Bachelors Degree	2	2	2	1	2	9	Low Risk	Proceed
Masters Degree	3	2	2	1	1	9	Low Risk	Proceed
Doctorate Degree	2	1	1	1	1	6	High Risk	Postpone
Six Sigma Black Belt	3	1	2	1	1	8	Average	Caution
Leadership Certification	2	1	1	1	1	6	High Risk	Postpone
Technical Certification	2	2	2	1	2	9	Low Risk	Proceed

Avg Score	2.3	1.5	1.7	1.0	1.3
Risk Level	Low Risk	High Risk	High Risk	High Risk	High Risk

Max Risk	5
Lowest Risk	11
Avg Risk	8

Figure 11.1   Risk Assessment Tool: Leadership Credentials.

promotions, pay increases and other growth opportunities. These gains and benefits far outweighed the risks and cost of investment. In this scenario, the investment was a game changer.

On the other hand, leader 2 invested $200,000 in the listed credentials and only 50% of them were low risk. As with leader 1, the doctorate and Black Belt were average or above risk. Unfortunately, the leader's career trajectory was flat, and the high-risk credentials were not valued, not used and did not produce a return. Thus, the credentials were simply plaques on the wall and a bad investment.

Finally, leader 3 invested in the advanced leadership certification that cost $15,000 initially with other costs forthcoming. This credential was high risk based on Figure 11.1. As with leader 2, leader 3 failed to earn a return on this investment. The training and credential evolved into another plaque on the wall. Thus, the risk was not worth the investment.

Summary

What did we learn from the case study? One, leaders don't know what they don't measure. Ignorance is never bliss and can be very costly. Also, risk is a reality that must be considered. If risk is left unchecked, it will eventually impact the leader and organization unfavorably. Often, leaders perceive investments in credentials to be a sure bet. But, in reality, they or their organizations end up with buyer's remorse as the unsuspecting risks limit the value gained.

Two, not all credentials are a game changer for the leader. Often, credentials become just another plaque on the wall. Thus, it's imperative that leaders risk assess learning opportunities to determine if they are truly a value added opportunity or just a waste of time. The adage of 'choose wisely' applies here. One of the greatest pitfalls of talent management is training for the sake of training. It's a costly proposition to the leader, organization and customer base.

Three, credentials can be beneficial if leveraged properly. Leadership accolades can provide new growth opportunities, more money, promotions and the like with time. The key is to measure and ensure the probability of success is greater than the actual direct costs.

In summary, investing in leadership credentials can be a risky proposition if not handled correctly. Leaders must leverage the four dimensions as noted in Figure 11. The end goal is to ensure the credential adds value to the leader, organization and customer base. Those credentials that have the greatest reach and probability of adding benefits to all stakeholders are the safest bet. In contrast, training for the sake of training results in a wall full of plaques that only collect dust.

References

1. Wikipedia. Credential. 2021. https://en.wikipedia.org/wiki/Credential
2. Investopedia. Opportunity cost. 2021. www.investopedia.com/terms/o/opportunitycost.asp

Chapter 12

Risk Assessing Leadership Burnout: Is the Tank Full or Running on Fumes?

Burnout

Burnout is 'a state of emotional, physical, and mental exhaustion caused by excessive and prolonged stress' (1). Leadership burnout is synonymous with being overwhelmed, overworked, overstressed and the like. Is burnout a healthy condition that motivates leaders to perform better? The short answer is no.

Is it possible for leaders to become burned out in their role? Does quality of life play a role in burnout? Do excessive stress, workloads and emotional instability play a role in leadership burnout? Is burnout a high-risk proposition for leaders and their customers? Is it possible to risk assess leadership burnout to predict its impact on the organization and its stakeholders? Can leaders become burned out due to boredom or lack of career challenges? We answer these and other considerations in the sections that follow.

The key is that leadership burnout is not good. It must be identified as early as possible, prevented when possible and addressed quickly. It's imperative that organizations view their leaders as people. Thus, people are not machines, and organizations must view each leader as a whole person. This simply means to ensure the whole person is healthy, engaged, taken care of and understood. Otherwise, leaders will quickly shift from a healthy working environment to one in which they are simply running on fumes.

DOI: 10.4324/9781003335108-13

Figure 12   Levels of Leadership Burnout.

For this conversation, we focus on three levels of leadership burnout. These levels include the role, the organization and the industry. See Figure 12 for details.

Role burnout occurs when one becomes burned out with a specific role. There are various causes for this level of burnout. The key is that the person is reasonably satisfied with the organization and industry they work in but have grown dissatisfied with the role. Common causes may include work–life balance, work schedules, leadership, working environments, coworkers, workloads and the like.

In contrast, there is the possibility of leaders becoming burned out with the organization. This too is multifactorial, but for simplicity, causes of organizational burnout may be leadership, culture, values, norms and the like. Moreover, leaders may become burned out with an industry. In their minds, the industry has run its course from their career perspective and the only fix is a career change.

There are also several dimensions of leadership burnout worth noting briefly. See Figure 12.1 for details.

The first dimension is environment. Burnout can occur by environmental factors. These attributes include stability, change levels and length of time changes are present. Common considerations are as follows: Is the environment riddled with high change, average change or low change? How long has the change lasted? What part of the organization or industry has been impacted by the change? A general rule of thumb is the greater the change is and the longer it lasts, the greater the chance for leadership burnout.

The second dimension of burnout is performance. Common considerations are as follows: Has the leader's performance improved? Is the leader's performance stagnant or declining? Has the leader mastered their craft and lack stimuli in the role to do better? Generally speaking, performance declines can be a good indicator that leaders are having issues and need help.

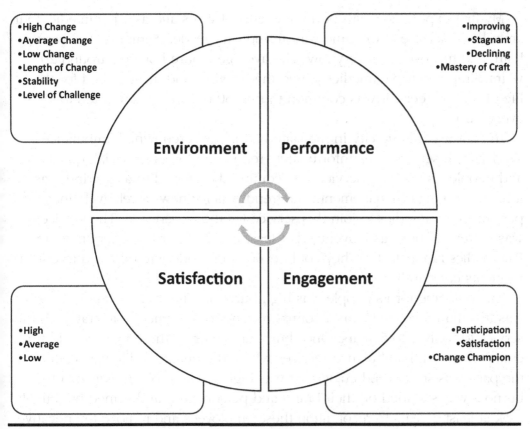

Figure 12.1   Dimensions of Leadership Burnout.

The third dimension is engagement. The key is that the higher the leadership engagement, the better. Organizations should consider several attributes here. Is the leader's participation the same as it was, declining or improving? Is the leader satisfied with the current role, the organization and the industry? Is the leader a change champion or a resistor of change? Irrespective of the attribute, the ideal state is when leaders are engaged and championing new ways of doing business. If the contrary is present, then more consideration is warranted.

The fourth dimension of leadership burnout is satisfaction. Is the leader's satisfaction high, medium or low? Again, satisfaction applies to the role, organization and industry. More often than not, highly satisfied leaders will perform better, stay longer and have a positive influence on the organization. It's imperative for organizations to consider routine employee satisfaction surveys to gauge acceptable levels of satisfaction versus crisis situations. Leaders simply don't know what they don't measure. Thus, keeping the finger on the leader satisfaction pulse is a good idea.

My first experience with burnout occurred years ago as a paramedic. Our ambulance service at the time was an industry leader. Seniority was very high, and turnover was very low. The average tenure hovered around 20 years. Simply put, paramedics joined this service, and most served for the life of their careers. It was common to find 30 or more years of tenure at every turn.

In contrast, a large city in the state had its own renowned ambulance service. The service was unfortunately renowned for its financial, quality and people issues. This service was commonly referred to as a grinder as it relates to talent management. The trend was for new or relatively inexperienced paramedics to join this service for the experience. The service was extremely busy as it averaged at least one call per hour per ambulance. Paramedics ran as fast as they could every shift and were exposed to critical incidents constantly.

The outcome for its people was high burnout. The average tenure for staff was less than 5 years. It was a common trend for paramedics to stay with the service for only 2 to 5 years. Once burnout occurred, these flyers would find employment with ambulance services where the quality of life was better, the pace was slower and enjoyment was higher. The problem was that the burnout was stamped on their brand and personalities and shined brightly. It took at least 2 years to recondition these employees and remove the negative attributes that occurred because of burnout.

The lessons learned are as follows: One, burnout is real and impacts all types of workers. Two, burnout can have long-term effects that will impact the person, organizations and all stakeholders. Three, it is possible to recondition burned-out leaders so they can enjoy their jobs, regain high productivity and have long-term successful employment. Finally, burnout can be avoided if leaders and organizations are proactive and take care of their people.

Another example occurred during the COVID-19 pandemic. When the pandemic hit the US, the world seemed to stop for a brief moment. Then, everyone was in emergency mode to respond and mitigate its effects. One health system followed the industry trend by invoking its emergency response command center. The command center was running nonstop for months on end—the longest in the organization's history.

Leaders who staffed the command center were inundated daily with problems, questions and new challenges never seen before. What most leaders thought would last for a few weeks lasted well over a year. Leaders quickly became overwhelmed and fatigued and could not see a brighter tomorrow up ahead.

As a result, leaders began retiring at record pace. Also, a new trend emerged where leaders began taking medical leave to deal with the side effects of this overwhelming persistent new state of operations. In particular, several long, tenured, very critical leaders abruptly resigned to find other roles in less stressful and more rewarding environments.

The consequences to the organization were long lasting and far reaching. This loss of knowledge and experience was devastating. The question no one asked is, 'Was this preventable?' A thought leader posed this question to senior leaders and offered a simple tool to risk assess leadership burnout potential. See Figure 12.2 for details.

Figure 12.2 is a simple risk assessment tool. The organization engaged the thought leader for an assessment of its leadership cadre. The purpose was to identify high-risk roles that were in the crosshairs of leadership burnout and then find innovative ways to prevent, mitigate and resolve burnout so leaders were healthier, happier and more satisfied with their roles, performed better and stayed longer.

As noted in the figure, the thought leader started with a small sample of top leaders. These leaders represented critical functions of the organization. If they left or went out on leave, a crisis would ensue. Each leader was scored on engagement, participation, performance outcomes, satisfaction and the work environment. In short, lower scores equaled higher risk. The less engaged, participatory and satisfied, the higher was the risk. Moreover, those leaders who had worked in high change areas for longer periods of time and noticed performance declines were at higher risk for burnout than their counterparts.

The results were shocking to say the least. Sixty percent of the leaders assessed were at high risk for burnout. Only one of the leaders was an average risk for burnout, and 20% were low risk. The organization was playing high-risk poker with its people and didn't know it.

When viewing Figure 12.2 vertically for each attribute, engagement and leadership participation were high risk. The takeaway is that burnout is a risky proposition, and the organization had no idea how close it was to losing more critical leaders. Thus, ignorance is never bliss.

The organization responded by addressing each leader individually. First, top leaders set a goal to learn as much as possible about the whole person. How were they feeling? Did they have off-the-job challenges that would negatively impact their work life? Were there any stressors that could be immediately improved and so on?

Next, the organization took great effort to focus on the small things. These solutions included recognizing leaders regularly for their dedication

Leader	Leader Engagement 1- Complacent 2- Neutral 3- Engaged	Performance Outcomes 1-Declined 2-Stagnant 3-Improving	Leader Participation 1-Resist Change 2-Favor Status Quo 3-Sponsor Change	Organizational Environment 1-High Change 2-Average Change 3-No Change	Leader Satisfaction 1-Low 2-Average 3-High	Risk Score *Sum Columns 2-6 Lower Score = Higher Risk	Risk Level
Leader 1	1	1	1	1	1	5	High Risk
Leader 2	3	2	2	1	1	9	High Risk
Leader 3	2	2	2	2	2	10	Average
Leader 4	3	1	2	1	1	8	High Risk
Leader 5	3	3	3	3	3	15	Low Risk

Avg Score	2.4	1.8	2.0	1.6	1.6	
Risk Level	High Risk	Low Risk	High Risk	Low Risk	Low Risk	

Max Risk	5
Lowest Risk	15
Avg Risk	10

Figure 12.2 Risk Assessment Tool: Leadership Burnout.

and persistence during the crisis. These recognitions were public, infor-mal and tailored to each individual leader to add a personal touch. The enterprise also adjusted work schedules based on feedback from leaders to enhance the quality of life and leadership satisfaction. Greater levels of autonomy were given to leaders, which provided flexibility in work routines.

Finally, the organization provided various financial incentives and reward to those high-risk leaders. Those in the crosshairs of burnout were rewarded for their due diligence and persistence. The incentives took the form of cash payouts, pay raises, food gift cards and so on. The key is the organization leveraged the identified risks to learn as much as they could about the current state. Then, the organization utilized this insight to pro-vide human solutions that would prevent, mitigate and overcome leadership burnout.

Summary

What did we learn from the case study? One, risk is a reality. The adage 'ignorance is bliss' is simply not true. Ignorance is never bliss. We live in a high-risk world that is always changing. As change grows, so will risk. The real question is simple, 'How will organizations and their leaders know their risk position if they don't measure risk?' Simply put, they won't.

Two, leaders are people and have human needs. Burnout is a reality that must be addressed proactively by organizations. As burnout occurs, many unfavorable attributes emerge as noted in Figure 12.2. The key is for leaders to know their risks and respond accordingly. The kryptonite for leadership burnout is rooted in understanding the whole person. Otherwise, ignorance will be bliss until disruption arrives.

Finally, it is possible to predict risks of burnout. A simple risk assessment is worth its weight in gold if utilized correctly. Risk of burnout is multi-dimensional. Thus, leaders need to paint a broad picture of risk so all facets are captured. The risk assessment tool simply provides signals that organiza-tions and their leaders are either running on a full tank of gas or on fumes. The ideal state is to constantly refill the tank so one is not left sitting on the side of the road, operationally speaking.

In summary, risk matters and has real impacts on humanity. Leaders simply don't know what they don't measure. Also, ignorance is never bliss. Leadership burnout is a risky proposition and is multifaceted. Effective lead-ers are those who proactively assess, understand and resonate with leaders as a whole person. Those who can master the leadership environment, engagement and satisfaction will ensure the tank never runs out of gas.

Reference

1. HelpGuide. *Burnout Prevention and Treatment*. 2021. www.helpguide.org/articles/stress/burnout-prevention-and-recovery.htm

---

Chapter 13

Risk Assessing Leadership Outcomes: Are We On Track or Off Target?

Determinants of Outcomes

Merriam-Webster defines outcomes as 'Something that follows as a result or consequence.' The concept of outcomes is synonymous with terms such as results, consequences, effects, aftermath, conclusion, product and the like (1). The key is that outcomes have both positive and negative connotations.

The litmus test for outcomes is if they produce value. Value is essentially anything a customer is willing to pay for (2). Often, leaders and their organizations perceive value in improvement with key performance indicators (KPIs) tied to service, cost and quality. This is a good starting point, but value is broader.

If a leader performs well and exceeds revenue expectations, is this a value added? If leaders improve wait times for patients in an emergency room, is this considered to add value? Simply put, yes. The takeaway is if leadership outcomes positively impact the customer, they are considered value added.

This begs further consideration. Are outcomes the truest test of a leader's worth? Is perception always reality? Is ignorance bliss or a one-way ticket on the disruption train? Does goal attainment mean all is well? Can a leader's performance be out of control even though the leader is meeting goals? Are leadership outcomes a risky business? Is it possible to risk assess leadership

DOI: 10.4324/9781003335108-14

performance to predict the future? Are there various levels of leadership outcomes? We answer these and other considerations in the sections that follow.

Levels of Outcomes

To start, thought leaders must consider four levels of performance outcomes. See Figure 13 for details.

The first level of leadership outcomes relates to the individual. When organizations are determining if leaders are adding value with performance, the first lens focuses on the individual. Simply put, is the individual leader meeting all operational KPIs for the role? If not, what percentage of goals are met weekly, monthly and annually? The goal is for individual leaders to meet more goals now and in the future.

The second level of outcomes is the department. Regardless of organizational type or industry, organizations are composed of business units or departments. If a department has five leaders, the enterprise here would focus on the bigger picture. Is the department meeting all its operational KPI goals? If not, what percentage of goals are being met each week, month and year?

The third level is divisional or in some instances entity goals. Think of a large health system, for example. The system is composed of ten hospitals. In order to manage effectively, leaders divide the hospital into five divisions based on scope, size and complexity of services.

The key for divisional outcomes is to determine what percentage of goals are being met weekly, monthly and annually. Does a common theme keep appearing? Are all KPIs meeting target? If not, what are the burning issues missing the mark?

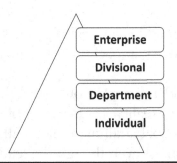

Figure 13   Levels of Performance.

The final level of leadership performance is the enterprise level. The enterprise view is simply a thirty-thousand-foot view of overall organizational performance. Is the organization performing well or failing? A quick overview of KPIs tied to service, cost, quality and revenues is a good indicator of success or failure at a glance, but more analysis is required.

It's important to note that assessing outcomes is not rocket science. Leaders simply need to ask three questions:

- Are we meeting goal?
- Are we improving goal attainment?
- Is goal attainment in control?

If the answer to all three is yes, then smooth sailing. If not, the organization is off track and needs correction. More details on this topic are forthcoming.

Dimensions of Leadership Outcomes

As organizations review leadership performance, they must consider four dimensions of outcomes. See Figure 13.1 for details.

The first dimension of leadership performance is goal attainment. As previously discussed, there are a few considerations. One, is goal attainment for main KPIs high, average or low? How would one know? In short,

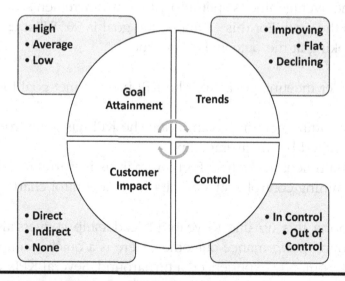

Figure 13.1   Dimensions of Leadership Performance.

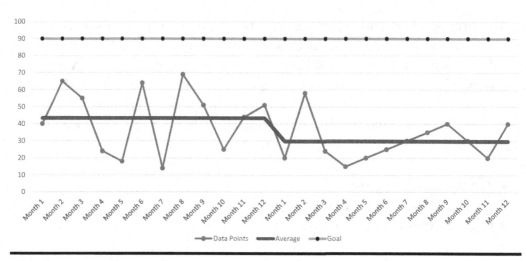

Figure 13.2   Run Chart.

leaders know what they measure. Thus, leaders must track goal attainment for respective KPIs frequently, over time periods, and watch for trends. See Figure 13.2 for a basic example.

Figure 13.2 is a basic run chart or line graph. The key here is there are three parts to consider. First, the dotted line represents the data points. For this example, it is monthly performance for the KPI. The line represents average goal attainment for the time period. Since the graph represents 24 months or 2 years, the leaders have chosen to compare each year to the next. Thus, the average line is split into 12-month increments.

The line is the goal. For this example, the goal is 90. What can one infer quickly by looking at the outcomes over time?

■ Is the leader meeting goal? No. The KPI has not met goal for the last 2 years.
■ Is the goal attainment improving? No. The KPI has gone from bad to worse as noted by the average line.
■ Is goal attainment in control? Further analysis is warranted. The method for determining control status of data is via a control chart, for example.

Side note: I bring this up due to years of leadership conversations that are misguided around performance outcomes. Here is a quick example. Recently, a large service company experienced a turnaround. Several KPIs were viewed by divisional and top leaders. The leaders noticed significant improvements in one major KPI that impacted the entire enterprise and hundreds of thousands of customers. Almost all the leaders viewed this as a celebration point—note 'almost all the leaders.'

One leader in the room viewed the run chart with several years of data and said, 'Your goal attainment is out of control.' Everyone in the room was confused, and you could have heard a pin drop. A thought leader said, 'How would you know?' The response was well thought out and a snare. Needless to say, the thought leader began to teach a very brief, impromptu and accelerated class to the leadership team on statistical process control (SPC).

The thought leader taught the divisional leader that a run chart is not the way to determine the control status of a KPI's performance. As an afterthought, the thought leader placed the data in a control chart. In short, the data were in control, and the improvements were significant. Thus, the team should have *all* celebrated the success. The divisional leader simply put their foot in their mouth in front of a group of senior leaders and peers. As the adage goes, 'ignorance is very dangerous and never bliss.'

As a reference of a sample control chart, see Figure 13.3.

The control chart has several parts, and this is just a sample chart. First, the dotted line represents, in this case, monthly goal attainment for a KPI. The line is the average of the data points. The lines (plural) represent upper and lower control limits. The purpose of this discussion is not to teach a statistical process control class.

Thus, let's keep it simple. The two data points above the top line indicate the outcomes are out of control. This is a signal that special cause

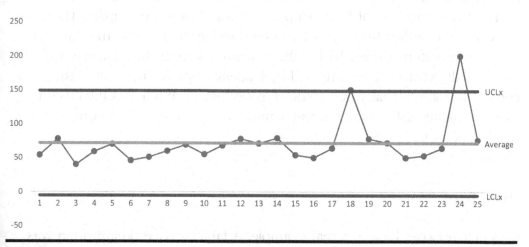

Figure 13.3 Control Chart.

variation is present. This signal is a clue for leaders to immediately go to where the work is being done to see where the process is being broken. If the control chart was in control and goal attainment was meeting or exceeding goal, then leaders would push full steam ahead.

The takeaway is that leaders don't know what they don't measure. Run charts and control charts are simple tools that tell a story at a glance. They can also give great insight into past, current and future performance outcomes if leveraged properly. The end goal is to display data over time and keep it simple.

Back to the main points. The second dimension of leadership outcomes is trends or data patterns. A starter for determining leadership performance as noted in Figure 13.2 is as follows:

- Are we meeting goal?
- Are we improving goal attainment?
- Is goal attainment in control?

At the end of the day, the goal is to meet more goals more frequently. Thus, leaders should always improve performance and ensure their outcomes are in control. If not, further consideration and analysis are warranted.

The third dimension of leadership performance is control. We discussed this in the previous example. All we need to say here is use a simple control chart often. If data are in control and meeting or exceeding goal, then stay on the tracks, and full steam ahead. If the control chart is out of control and the data are not moving in the right direction, go to the Gemba (2). The answer and correction can be found where the work is being done.

The last dimension of leadership outcomes is customer impact. There are a few considerations here as well as noted in Figure 13.1. Do the outcomes impact the customer directly? Do the outcomes impact the customer indirectly? Is the customer not affected by leadership performance and their outcomes? The key is that when leadership performance impacts the customer, they are higher risk. Thus, outcomes must be on target and in control. If not, risk levels soar.

Risk Tool

Let's take a closer look at a real example. A large service organization was experiencing operational declines for several years. The biggest declines in KPI goal attainment related to quality and finances. In short, for several years, the enterprise lost millions of dollars, and its quality unfavorably impacted thousands of customers. Thus, the organization was near insolvency, and a turnaround was warranted.

The top leadership team engaged a thought leader for assistance. The first step was a current state assessment to identify gaps, burning issues and performance opportunities. One aspect of the organizational review was a risk assessment tied to individual leadership goal attainment. See Figure 13.4 for details.

One top leader who 'appeared' to perform well for several years was chosen for a pilot study. The focus for the pilot was on KPIs related to value, such as cost, revenue, quality, employee engagement and turnover. The key is that these focal points either directly or indirectly impacted value to each customer.

The leader was scored on several attributes, including goal attainment, KPI trends, performance control and customer impact for the selected KPIs. As noted in the figure, the leader was high risk for 40% of KPIs including cost and employee engagement. Moreover, the leader's performance was average risk revenue and quality. Only employee turnover was low risk.

What does this mean? If this top leader was only performing well in 20% of the KPIs, what about the other hundreds of leaders? The key here is that the leader was marginal to high risk in performance outcomes. The adage of 'what sparkles doesn't always shine' applies here.

When viewing the figure horizontally for each attribute, the leader was also high risk for KPI trends, KPI control and the impact this performance had on the customer. In layman's terms, this leader's performance significantly impacted the customer base. Also, the performance was flat to declining and more often than not out of control. Thus, the variation and lack of dependability placed this leader as high risk to the organization and its customers. Was the leader on target or off track? Simply put, the performance outcomes were off the rails.

The team then used the same risk tool for subgroups of leaders in various divisions. They realized the performance issues were systemic and not just an anomaly with one leader. As noted in Figure 13.5, five top leaders were assessed. They represented the value equation (service, cost and quality) for the enterprise.

As noted in the figure, 40% of the leaders were high risk. They simply met fewer goals over time, the goal attainment had a lot of variation and these attributes highly impacted the customer base. Similarly, 40% of the

KPI	KPI Meeting Goal? 1- Not Meeting Goal 2- Meets Goal 3- Exceeds Goal	KPI Trend 1-Declining 2-Flat 3-Improving	Is KPI Performance in Control? 1-No 2-Yes	Impact 1-Directly Impacts Customer 2-Indirectly Impacts Customer 3-No Impact	Risk Score *Sum Columns 2-5 Lower Score = Higher Risk	Risk Level
Cost	1	1	1	1	4	High Risk
Revenue	3	2	2	1	8	Average
Quality	2	2	2	2	8	Average
Employee Engagement	3	1	2	1	7	High Risk
Turnover	3	3	1	3	10	Low Risk
Avg Score	2.4	1.8	1.6	1.6		
Risk Level	Low Risk	High Risk	High Risk	High Risk		
Max Risk	4					
Lowest Risk	11					
Avg Risk	8					

Figure 13.4 Risk Assessment Tool: Individual Leader Performance.

Leader	KPI Meeting Goal? 1- Not Meeting Goal 2- Meets Goal 3- Exceeds Goal	KPI Trend 1-Declining 2-Flat 3-Improving	Is KPI Performance in Control? 1-No 2-Yes	Impact 1-Directly Impacts Customer 2-Indirectly Impacts Customer 3-No Impact	Risk Score *Sum Columns 2-5 Lower Score = Higher Risk	Risk Level
Leader 1	1	1	1	1	4	High Risk
Leader 2	3	2	2	1	8	Average
Leader 3	3	3	1	3	10	Low Risk
Leader 4	2	2	2	2	8	Average
Leader 5	2	1	1	3	7	High Risk
Avg Score	2.2	1.8	1.4	2.0		
Risk Level	Low Risk	High Risk	High Risk	High Risk		

Max Risk 4
Lowest Risk 11
Avg Risk 8

Figure 13.5   Risk Assessment Tool: Multiple Leader Performance.

leaders were average risk. They too had performance outcomes issues with KPI goal attainment trends, variation and customer impact. Only one of the leaders in the sample was low risk and on target.

Viewing Figure 13.5 vertically, the same pattern existed as was discovered in Figure 13.4 with the first leader. The organization was high risk overall with goal attainment trends, control and customer impact. These attributes warranted the greatest attention. The solution is for the enterprise to find leaders who can meet more goals more consistently, constantly improve and enhance value to the customer base.

The lesson learned is that the organization's performance issues were multifocal and not sustainable. Business as usual was a dead-end road. This insight resulted in leadership changes, an organizational restructure and a new strategic direction. The adage of 'out with the old and in with the new' applied here.

Summary

What did we learn from the case study and discussion? One, perception is not always reality. There are several adages that apply here: 'All pop, no fizz.' 'What sparkles doesn't always shine.'

'A diamond in the rough may simply be a lump of coal when exposed.' The key is that leaders and their organizations don't know what they don't measure. Ignorance is never bliss and can be very dangerous. Thus, leaders must objectively measure performance and outcomes to see the true picture. Otherwise, we are heroes in our own minds.

Two, outcomes are arguably the truest test of a leader's worth. There is an art and a science to leading people. Leadership is the art of getting people to do what you want without force. The art is influencing people, while the science is objective data from outcomes. In the end, both must align, be significant and show improvement in the long term. Otherwise, leadership capital is less than expected, less than advertised and will evaporate quickly.

Three, leadership performance is a risky business. Change is the new normal and only constant. As change increases, so does risk. Thus, leaders must risk assess their outcomes, performance and the value they add or take away from the organization and its stakeholders.

In summary, risk and leadership outcomes are important. Leadership is a risky business. Often, what leaders perceive to be an oasis is discovered to be a mirage once risk assessed. The end goal is for leaders to meet more goals more consistently over time. Effective leaders are those who can lead people, constantly produce high-performing outcomes and keep the train racing full steam ahead down the track. Poor leadership outcomes are a sure bet for the train to derail sooner rather than later.

References

1. Merriam-Webster. Outcome. 2021. www.merriam-webster.com/dictionary/outcome#synonyms
2. Institute of Industrial and Systems Engineers (IISE), Lean Green Belt, 2016.

Chapter 14

Leveraging Risk to Find the Right Fit: Remote or In-Person Work?

The Change Environment

One of the biggest challenges leaders face in a post–COVID-19 work environment is determining which roles should be onsite versus remote. When the pandemic arrived to the US in 2020, remote work for many industries was taboo. The traditional operating model in many organizations was for staff and leaders to report daily to a brick-and-mortar location. Some traditional leaders perceived onsite work as the sure bet to ensure productivity, accountability and quality of work met its peak.

As the pandemic spread across the world, a lot of the norms of yesteryears were disrupted. For example, the shakings impacted financial markets, the travel industry, healthcare, geopolitics and essentially every aspect of human life. In healthcare, for example, some large organizations sent 10% to 30% of the workforce home to work remotely, thus breaking long-vetted traditions and perceptions of how work 'could' be done in this industry.

As the world has adjusted to this new operating environment, leaders are being forced to make permanent talent management decisions around work locations. There are typically three decision points. What roles can work remotely some of the time? What roles must work onsite all the time? What roles can work remotely all the time?

DOI: 10.4324/9781003335108-15

The role taglines have evolved to 'onsite,' 'hybrid' and 'remote' work roles. The key here is that a specific decision on role category will be organization and industry specific. Leaders will have to ensure the path ahead meets organizational, industry and regulatory requirements, but decisions will be required by many industries.

Keeping that in mind, there are several considerations for leaders not to overlook. Can remote work provide hard dollar savings to both the organization and employee? Can remote work options be an employee satisfier and improve engagement? Is all remote work a non-value-added prospect? Is remote work a risky proposition or a sure bet? Will all roles fit a remote work structure? Can a simple risk assessment tool help leaders make tough talent management decisions easily? We answer these and other questions in the sections that follow.

Case in Point

Recently, two examples of leveraging risk to find the right role work location emerged. The first example relates to a manufacturing organization. A thought leader in the manufacturing industry was faced with making such decisions. The organization had thousands of workers.

Traditionally, all staff and leaders worked onsite. This was the norm and the time-tested battle proven strategy for many tenured leaders. As COVID-19 emerged, thousands of staff and leaders were sent home to work remotely. Initially, the fear was productivity, quality of work and engagement would plummet.

As time passed, the leaders realized many remote staff and leaders were as productive as or more productive than before. Moreover, satisfaction rates of many remote workers skyrocketed. These 'at-home' roles afforded them more time with family and friends and saved countless hours and money in not having to travel daily to a fixed location. Thus, value was added at every turn.

As time passed, the organization hit a crossroad. Organizational leaders were forced to make permanent decisions as to what roles would return to onsite work versus work remotely. A 'clash of the titans' scenario emerged. Younger and forward-thinking leaders were proponents of remote work as operational metrics actually improved since these attributes were instituted.

In contrast, traditional leaders were opposed to the thought of paying employees to work from home permanently. The 'out of sight, out of mind' perspective ruled here. The traditional leaders simply struggled with the fact that they could not directly monitor employees if they could not see them. Is this a shortsighted view? Many argued that it was.

A second example is similar and relates to the healthcare industry. As the pandemic hit the US, a large health system sent thousands of staff and leaders home to work remotely for an undetermined time. The philosophy was simple. Take things a day at a time and pivot as needed.

As time passed, the organization's leaders were forced to make permanent decisions related to work assignments. To help with these inflection points, teams were assembled to study roles and reporting structures. Moreover, the organization sent waves of surveys out to leaders and staff working remotely to gauge productivity and engagement levels of this new talent management paradigm.

As with the manufacturing organization, the health system realized positive impacts of remote work. Many roles were more productive and more satisfied working remotely. The enterprise also realized hard dollar savings to both the institution and its employees with the injection of remote work. But, the detractors also emerged. Traditionalists supported the perspective of bringing everyone back to onsite work.

The reality was that both organizations spent countless hours and a lot of money assessing their organizations, debating options, surveying employees and simply arguing over competing perspectives. The question is why? Are customers willing to pay for all this activity? Does this process add value to the customer? In short, this activity seemed productive. But, it's easy to argue that it was a non-value-added activity and only added confusion to the situation. Let's look closer.

Risk Tool

One of the simplest ways to make critical decisions quickly is with a risk tool. Figure 14 outlines a simple risk assessment for this topic of onsite versus remote work.

Leaders start by listing the roles in question for consideration. As noted, each role is scored as if it has the potential to work remotely all the time, some of the time or none of the time. Some roles are simply not a good fit for remote work and require an onsite presence always. Think of a nurse working in an emergency room, for example.

Next, leaders score each role on productivity. If the role is shifted to a remote work site, will it produce more, less or the same productivity as working onsite? Considerations are also given for dollar savings if the role is remote versus onsite. There are two perspectives here: employee and organization. The simple perspective is if the role conversion to remote work will save the organization or employee money.

Each role is then scored on employee satisfaction and business impact. Will remote work increase, decrease or have a neutral impact on employee job satisfaction? Also, will remote work provide operational benefits that will ultimately impact the customer? Once scoring is complete, the tool calculates a risk score. In this model, lower scores equate to lower risk. Thus, lower scoring roles are a better fit for remote work.

Let's take a more practical look at Figure 14.1. An organization is assessing three roles to determine if each will be a better fit for onsite, remote or hybrid work structure. Role 1 represents an employee who processes bills electronically daily. This role can work remotely all the time and increases productivity if shifted to a remote location. Also, employees are more satisfied working remotely, and this option provides hard dollar savings in office space and driving time. The impact on business operations is an improvement due to higher engagement and satisfaction of the workforce. Thus, this role is a good fit for remote work.

Role 2 is a consultant who guides organizational leaders in performance improvement, cost savings and other thought leadership topics. This role requires some in-person interaction with organizational leaders, but much of the work can be done remotely. With a hybrid role, productivity and business impact will stay the same. Moreover, there are no dollar savings if the role is shifted to remote work only. Thus, it's an average fit for remote work. This means the organization would be best served to keep this a hybrid role.

Role 3 is a nurse in an emergency department. This role is required to be onsite for obvious reasons. Also, moving this role to remote would provide little to no benefit to the organization. Thus, it's a poor fit for remote work.

Impact Calculator

When making organizational decisions, particularly those that involve time and money, leaders may need to consider using a simple impact calculator. See Figure 14.2 for details.

As noted in Figure 14.2, there are three scenarios impacted by remote work decisions. The first entails employee miles driven to work. The

Role	Can the role work remotely? 1- All the time 2- Some of the time 3- None of the time	Productivity if the role is remote? 1-More productive 2- Same as in person 3- Less productive	Dollar savings to organization if role is remote? 1- Yes 2- No	Employee or Leader Satisfaction of working remotely? 1- More Satisfied 2- Average 3- Less Satisfied	Business Impact (Benefit Potential) 1- Improve Operations 2- Neutral to Operations 3- Negative Impact on Operations	Risk Score *Sum Columns 2-6 Lower Score = Lower Risk	Fit With Remote Work
Role 1	1	1	1	1	1	5	Good Fit
Role 2	2	2	2	2	2	10	Average Fit
Role 3	3	3	2	3	3	14	Poor Fit

Figure 14.1 Risk assessment tool

Employee Miles Driven to Work

Daily Miles Driven to Work Roundtrip (Average)	Fleet Cost Per Mile	Daily Savings Per Employee	Annual Savings Per Employee	Annual Savings 100 Employees	Annual Savings 200 Employees
60	$0.50	$30.00	$7,500.00	$750,000.00	$1,500,000.00

Employee Time Driving to Work

Employee Time Spent Driving Roundtrip (Hrs)	Average Hourly Rate ($)	Daily Savings Per Employee	Annual Savings Per Employee	Annual Savings 100 Employees	Annual Savings 200 Employees
2	$25.00	$50.00	$12,500.00	$1,250,000.00	$2,500,000.00

Office Space (Foot Print)

Office Amenities Per Office($)	$ Savings by Eliminating 100 Offices	$ Savings by Eliminating 200 Offices	$ Savings by Eliminating 300 Offices
$2,500.00	$250,000.00	$500,000.00	$750,000.00

Figure 14.2   The reality is that decisions have impact and are costly, but leaders often fail to assess, analyze or leverage this knowledge in decision-making.

decision to allow employees to work remotely has a monetary impact on the employee's wallet from miles driven back and forth to work daily. If an average employee drives 60 miles to work round trip daily, it could easily cost $30 per day in fleet costs.

Fleet costs represent fuel, brakes, oil changes and the like. Simply put, these are global transportation costs for employees to transit to work daily. Over the course of the year, the employee will save $7,500 if allowed to work remotely. Annually, 100 employees would collectively save $750,000. The takeaway is that a simple but important decision will have significant cost savings impacts on the organization's employees. Thus, this consideration and analysis are warranted.

The second scenario in Figure 14.1 relates to time employees spend driving to work and the associated costs. If an average employee drives 60 miles per day round trip to a fixed location, this may equate to 2 hours of driving time (market dependent). Considering the average hourly salary cost, the daily savings would be $50 in Figure 2's example. Annually, the savings would be over $12,000. For 100 employees, the dollar savings collectively would be over $1,000,000.

The third scenario relates to savings in office space as a result of transitioning employees to remote work. Offices can be an expensive venture for many reasons. For simplicity, let's focus on amenities such as furniture, phones, decorations, copiers, computers and the like. If the average office space requires $2,500 in amenities as noted in Figure 14.1, the organization could save $500,000 per year if 300 employees were transitioned to remote work. There are many other considerations such as property taxes, rent, utilities, facilities management costs and the like. The purpose of this exercise is to start the creative thinking process.

The key here is simplicity. In the previous examples, organizations and their leaders spent countless hours and money debating role assignments. They also struggled to see the forest for the trees. Each decision has consequences on all affected stakeholders. In reality, a simple tool would help make critical decisions very quickly, thus adding value at every turn and alleviating emotional debates and conflict.

Also, an impact calculator would make leadership perspectives clearer and decisions more stakeholder-centric. Did anyone stop to ask why engagement with some employees increased while working remotely? Did they consider the dollar savings in driving and transportation each employee saved? Did they consider the organization's footprint and associated savings of remote work? Irrespectively, the takeaway is that decisions are multifaceted, have impact, are laden with risk and require multiple lenses to capture the right perspectives.

Summary

In today's world, change is the new norm and only constant. The reality is that change has associated risks and consequences. As it relates to work roles, leaders must ensure they have the right perspective when determining how to manage talent. The key is to leverage simple risk tools and impact calculators to ensure logic overrides emotional decision-making.

Simple decisions such as allowing workers to work from nontraditional sites can save all stakeholders a lot of time, money and inconvenience. If managed properly, these emerging operating models can also add value at every turn and provide less risky options for service delivery. The harsh reality is that leaders don't know what they don't measure. Those who master the art of assessment, measurement, analysis and risk mitigation will thrive. In contrast, those leaders who continue to follow traditional paths and emotion-filled decision-making will simply die on the vine.

In summary, leadership is an art and a science. Effective leaders are those who can successfully manage relationships to drive significant outcomes. Outcomes are predicated on leaders cultivating the right organizational culture. Achieving the right fit in talent management, work roles and risk is the key to ensuring organizational longevity and market dominance.

Chapter 15

When the Early Bird Misses the Worm: Signals of When to Promote, Not to Promote and Transition Leaders Out

Introduction

In today's world, change is the only constant, but it seems the level, nature and frequency of change are increasing over time. Change occurs when some attribute alters the current state. Formally, change can be defined as 'To give a different position, course, or direction to' (1). Change can be related to people, operations, leadership, organizational culture, strategic planning and any other aspect of running a business.

From a leadership perspective, it's important to consider change relevant to promotions and forced leadership changes. As the market has shifted from traditional to transformational, leaders must decide wisely who will run the organization or exit leadership roles. One of the biggest pitfalls deciding leaders make is to promote someone before they are ready or promote them to the wrong role. Moreover, the decision to transition leaders out of their current roles is a major decision leaders cannot take lightly.

As change evolves and intensifies, so will the risk to organizations. Risk as it relates to this conversation can be defined as, 'Someone or something that creates or suggests a hazard' (2). As risk grows, so must the

DOI: 10.4324/9781003335108-16

organization's response to various foci. Ignorance is not bliss. Thus, leaders can only mitigate, prevent or respond to issues they are aware of.

There are several considerations leaders must entertain when making leadership selection or transition decisions. Is it possible to risk assess organizational leaders? Is it possible to predict the potential success or failure of leaders (both current and aspiring) with a simple risk assessment? Will this promotion lead to more or less risk for the enterprise? Is the current leadership cadre high or low risk of failure? If certain leaders are transitioned out of the enterprise, will this decision create more or less risk for the organization? These and many other considerations are addressed in the sections that follow.

For years, people have used the adage 'the early bird gets the worm.' This phrase is typically synonymous with being proactive, a self-starter, a hard worker and the like. Related to making leadership decisions, this phrase has more significance than most may realize. If leaders are not proactive with risk assessments, knee-jerk reactions to promote or transition leaders to other roles can quickly lead to unintended consequences. Thus, the bird misses the worm as quick decisions are not well thought out or simply high risk.

Let's take a closer look at a case study that covers these topics in depth and will provide more insight.

Case Study

Recently, a very large service organization experienced top leadership change. The new leader came in and engaged in a clean sweep of the top leadership team. The intent was to add skill sets and perspectives to catapult the enterprise from a traditional operating model to a transformational paradigm. The end goal was to ensure the enterprise was high performing and a national best practice site for years to come.

Historically, the organization was relatively high performing in core business outcomes. Shortly after the clean sweep was implemented, the organization realized a short-lived uptick in operational performance. Soon after, organizational chaos ensued, and operational outcomes tied to service, financials and quality of services tanked. Initially, the enterprise was meeting over 70% of its operational goals. Post restructure, the organization was meeting less than 50% of its goals tied to quality, service and financials for consecutive years running.

You may be wondering why this is significant? The organizational impact was disastrous. The knee-jerk reaction led to a loss of hundreds of millions of dollars. Moreover, service declines impacted several hundred thousand customers annually and posed immediate risks to life, safety and health. Over a very short period, the organization transitioned from a very stable financial position to being insolvent.

The real consideration relates to why? In retrospect, a team was assembled to study the decisions and subsequent outcomes. Step one was to risk assess the newly formed top leadership cadre. See Figure 15 for details.

The results were eye opening. As noted in Figure 15, the newly assembled leadership team was risk assessed on four factors. First, each leader was assessed based on their skill set. Did the leader have technical, operations and performance improvement experience with measurable outcomes? If yes, they were rated as yes. If they only possessed one or two of the skill sets, then they were rated as no.

Second, the leaders were rated as to if they had achieved cross-functional wins. This simply means, were they successful in improving 'something' operationally in an area outside of their base training or comfort zone. Those leaders with cross-functional wins received a 1. Their counterparts who did not have wins outside their business unit receive a 2.

The next two attributes are related. The question here is did the leaders produced performance improvement outcomes in any arena that were statistically significant? Moreover, did those significant outcomes get published in a respected industry venue? The same yes or no measure was used here as well.

Finally, the sum score for columns 2–5 produced a risk score. The key here, as noted in Figure 15, is that lower scores are better. Ideally, each leader would meet each requirement as listed, thus scoring a 4. Any score above the goal of 4 is considered high risk.

The team used the leadership risk assessment tool to score the top leadership group of enterprise leaders. For the cohort of nine leaders, only one of them had an integrated skill set composed of technical skills, operations experience and performance improvement expertise. All others had only one or two of these attributes. The adage 'one-trick pony' applies here.

The leadership cohort also did not have any cross-functional wins outside their business unit area of expertise. They may have been masters of their craft, but the impact was limited to their comfort zones. Moreover, the entire cohort did not have any significant performance improvement outcomes that were published. Thus, all leaders in the cohort were high-risk appointments.

Leader	Integrated Skill Set? (1=Yes; 2=No)	Cross Functional Wins (1=Yes; 2=No)	Published Outcomes (1=Yes; 2=No)	Performance Improvement Significant Outcomes (1=Yes; 2=No)	Risk Score *Sum Columns 2-5 Lower Score = Lower Risk	Ideal Goal
Leader 1	1	2	2	2	7	4
Leader 2	2	2	2	2	8	4
Leader 3	2	2	2	2	8	4
Leader 4	2	2	2	2	8	4
Leader 5	2	2	2	2	8	4
Leader 6	2	2	2	2	8	4
Leader 7	2	2	2	2	8	4
Leader 8	2	2	2	2	8	4
Leader 9	2	2	2	2	8	4

Figure 15 Leadership Role Risk Assessment Tool.

You may be wondering why this matters. First, the market had shifted from a traditional operating model to one that favored transformational attributes. This simply meant from a leadership perspective that new skills, impact and outcomes were required. In years past, this industry's leaders thrived with siloed skill sets. But, the new market required a diversified skill set portfolio. The leaders were simply not equipped to perform in a transformational environment. Thus, they were set up for failure unknowingly from the start.

Second, the leadership team was unifocal. They all scored the same or very close on every dimension. Does the term 'groupthink' resonate here? Groupthink occurs when everyone is similar in perspective or thought. This is very dangerous to the team dynamic. Ideally, teams should be composed of various skill sets, world views, capabilities and the like. This diversity of attributes helps teams avoid the mono approach to leading and making decisions. Groupthink created a comfortable environment for the team that led to a detrimental end. The adage 'ignorance is never bliss' applies here.

Finally, the early bird missed the worm. The new top leader had the best of intentions, but execution was a problem. It's reasonable to say that the risks with the clean sweep decision far outweighed the benefits of making a sudden knee-jerk reaction to restructure a top leadership team blindly. The takeaway is we don't know what we don't measure. What we don't know as leaders can have detrimental effects on the organization and all its stakeholders.

Summary

As noted, the only constant in today's world is change. As change persists, so will its associated risks. The only question is how many leaders will be able to see the forest for the trees? In other words, will leaders possess the capabilities and take the time to risk assess leadership decisions?

As we learned in the case study, risk can be detrimental to organizations, their leaders and ultimately all stakeholders including customers. Ignorance is never bliss. The key is to measure twice and cut once. Without assessing, measuring and analyzing the current state, leaders will be prone to making premature decisions that can sink the ship (operationally speaking).

In summary, it is possible to risk assess organizational leaders. Thought leaders should simply think through every risk before making leadership promotions or transitioning leaders out of their roles. It is also possible to predict the potential success or failure of leaders (both current and aspiring) with a simple risk assessment. As noted in Figure 1, if the top leader realized the mono nature of the newly assembled team beforehand, they may have reconsidered the clean sweep for a slower transition plan.

The key is to ensure current and future leaders possess the attributes to meet market, industry and customer requirements. Although groupthink may be comfortable to leaders, it's toxic in the long run and will inhibit long-term success. The end goal is for leaders to master risk assessment to ensure the early bird gets the worm.

References

1. Merriam-Webster. Change. 2021. www.merriam-webster.com/dictionary/change
2. Merriam-Webster. Risk. 2021. www.merriam-webster.com/dictionary/risk

Out With the Old, In With the New: Expected Roles of the Top Leader for the 2020s and Beyond

Introduction

Is leadership as easy as it seems? Are leadership roles overrated or worth the cost? Will leadership archetypes of the past work in today's disruptive market? If the market is evolving and being disrupted constantly, can top leaders stick to the old playbook and be successful in the long term? What roles must top leaders in today's market possess to be successful? We answer these and other questions in the sections that follow.

Leadership is essentially getting people to do what you want without force. Peter Drucker defines a leader as 'someone who has followers.' By definition, leadership can be defined as 'A process of social influence, which maximized the efforts of others, towards the achievement of a goal' (1). In layman's terms, a leader is one who can manage relationships to drive outcomes. Irrespective of how leaders are defined, the rules of the game have changed.

The healthcare industry, for example, has experienced some of the highest leadership disruption of top leaders recently. For nearly the last decade, hospital CEO rates have circled at almost 20% for consecutive years running (2). This simply means that two out of every ten top hospital leaders have or

DOI: 10.4324/9781003335108-17

will be disrupted. Looking back the last couple decades, this is the longest and highest sustained top leader disruption in recent history for this industry. The question is why?

Why are top leaders in healthcare being disrupted at such a high rate? Is this a fad or new normal? What will it take to quell the storm? Can this cycle be broken or is a new leadership archetype needed for the current environment? The short answer to these questions is simple. The market has changed and so must the top leaders who run the industry.

The Change Evolution

See Figure 16 for details. Figure 16 outlines a simple schematic of the market's journey from the traditional environment to the new transformational landscape.

Sticking with the healthcare industry example, for years the industry mainly experienced incremental change. This type of change is slow in nature, minimally disruptive and more manageable. Moreover, as noted in Figure 16, these incremental changes were typically segmented by time. This simply means that leaders and their organizations could plan for, react to and absorb change slowly over time. Thus, disruption levels were lower.

In contrast, Figure 16 also outlines the current change environment. In today's world, leaders and their organizations are experiencing waves of radical, cyclical and disruptive changes never seen before. Let's take a look at a few examples. For years, the healthcare industry has experienced rising costs and declining revenues. As time has passed, many organizations have struggled with financial solvency. Thus, record numbers of hospital mergers and acquisitions emerged as leaders attempted to alleviate those pressures.

As these pressures have mounted, the COVID-19 pandemic hit the nation concurrently. The pandemic increased costs and all but crippled the revenue streams for many hospitals and health systems across the country. Simply put, the pandemic added salt to an already gaping wound. These pressures, disruptions and radical changes have accelerated the disruptive nature of an already fragile industry. Thus, many top leaders have been forced into other roles or out of the industry. Consequently, top leadership turnover has increased with no sign of slowing down.

Recently, a large health system embarked on a simple study of its top leaders to determine how this disruptive market has, is and will affect their enterprise. The results and insight were surprising. Over a 5-year period, the

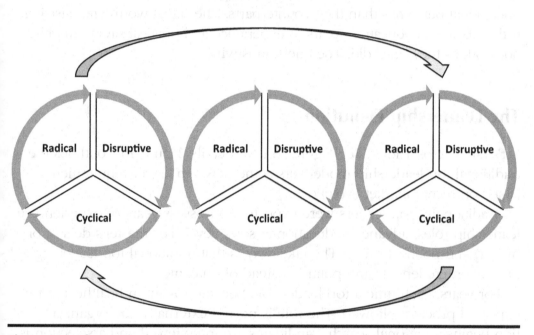

Figure 16 Change Environment.

enterprise experienced roughly a 30% turnover rate of top organizational leaders. This was obviously higher than the national average.

The enterprise discovered that the highest leadership turnover was in the C-Suite. This simply means the top leaders selected to run the organization strategically were leaving at a much higher rate than any other leadership group. Also, those leaders with the highest education levels (i.e., doctorate level) left at a much higher rate than their counterparts with a master's degree. Typically, those candidates with many years of industry experience, higher emotional intelligence levels and higher education levels had less sustained tenure (10 years or less).

In contrast, the organization realized that there was a long tenured group of leaders who consistently possessed greater than 10 years of employment with the enterprise. This tenured group of leaders exhibited interesting attributes that varied from their other top leader colleagues. The tenured leaders tended to have at most master's degrees, statistically significant operational outcomes with improvement and efficiency and only modest levels of emotional intelligence.

What does this really mean? The enterprise learned that as the market evolved, outcomes were more important than credentials. The leaders who stood the test of time were better at managing relationships to drive significant operational outcomes than their counterparts. The signal worth emphasizing is that advanced education, years of experience and political savvy simply did not work as they once did. The question is why?

The Leadership Evolution

Let's take a closer look. See Figure 16.1 for details. Figure 16.1 outlines the traditional top leadership model versus the new top leader requirements based on recent market evolutions.

Traditionally, top leaders were expected to possess years of experience in leadership roles, advanced education at some level (i.e., master's degree or higher) and political savvy. The takeaway is that traditional top leaders relied heavily on credentials and politics instead of outcomes.

For years, each time a top leader role became vacant in healthcare, the expected process followed. The role is posted externally, the organization begins a national search, candidates are interviewed and a selection is made. The tag line of years past has been, 'Please congratulate leader "x" on their new role as they have been found to be the best fit after an extensive search.' The real question relates to 'fit.' What does 'the best fit' really mean? Traditionally, 'the best fit' was tied to experience in certain roles, education and leadership presence (i.e., political savvy). Is this approach outdated? The short answer is yes.

In Figure 16.1, a basic outline of the new top leader model for basic requirements is greatly different from the traditional model. In today's world, a top leader's moxy is composed of several attributes, such as technical skills, operational outcomes, change agent mastery, relationship management and knowledge impact. Let's unpack these simply. Top leaders must now be

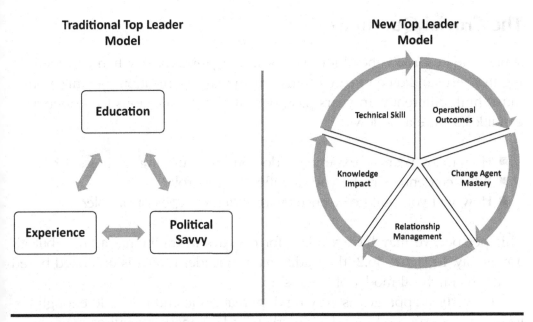

Figure 16.1   Leadership Requirements.

able to manage relationships in a way that produces signficant outcomes tied to service, quality, costs and efficiency as a starter.

But, how does one accomplish this in such a disruptive environment? Step one is that leaders will have to possess, cultivate and master change agent skills. If the market and industry are changing constantly, then change management is now the new minimum requirement for top leaders. An integrated skills set will help with this.

The new leader will have to possess technical skills, performance improvement knowledge with outcomes and operational prowess. For example, a healthcare top leader would need measureable experience and outcomes running an operation, clinical insight as to how the clinical side of the business operates and a change agent credential such as a Six Sigma Black Belt or the like with published wins. Morever, the new test of leadership mettle will be knowledge impact. Leaders must be able to show how they have signficantly impacted the industry body of knowledge and beyond. This knowledge sharing may take the form of publications, books, presentations at national industry venues and the like. Irrespectively, the new minimum for success is producing transformational outcomes in a transformational market.

The Crucial Questions

What's the best road ahead for leaders and organizations? When considering the best candidate to run a transformational organization, organizations must think differently. In years past, typical sample questions for leadership candidates were as follows:

- How many years of experience do you have running business 'x'?
- What credentials make you qualified for this role?
- How will you build consensus with different types of people?

This perspective may have worked for decades in traditional arenas, but it's a new day. In Figure 16.2, the traditional top leader model is exhibited based on the hierarchical model of leadership.

This vertical approach is very rigid, bureaucratic and not agile enough for top leaders to succeed in today's market. Today's market requires new considerations and a shift to a new paradigm.

In Figure 16.2, the new top leader model is very different from the traditional leadership archetype. Organizations should consider an outcomes-based questionnaire when considering top talent to fill crucial leadership roles. Common questions may include the following:

- Do you have technical, operational and change management skills?
  - If so, what results have you achieved in implementing transformational change in the last 12 months?
  - Are the results statistically significant, and have they been sustained?
  - Where has this work been published?
- How do you regularly impact the industry body of knowledge and beyond?
- How have you implemented large-scale change in the last 12 months?
  - If so, what were the key performance indicators (KPIs) selected for success?
  - Was the change successful and outcomes statistically significant?

Obviously, these are just a few thoughts to spark a creative and impactful conversation. Organizations and leaders must ensure that basic talent management laws and regulations are followed precisely. But, the key takeaway is that leadership archetypes of old will not be as effective as in the past. Leaders must pivot, evolve and chart a new course to remain viable in the long term.

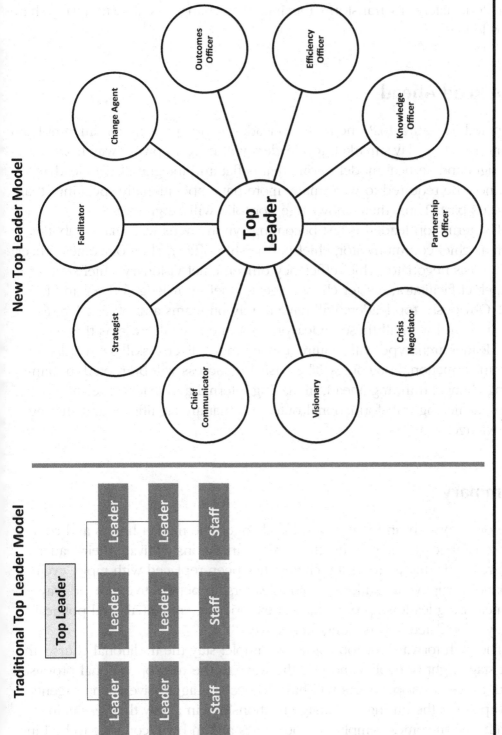

Traditional Top Leader Model

New Top Leader Model

Figure 16.2 Leadership Archetypes.

The million-dollar question all leaders must be prepared for is, 'What have you done lately' to transform the industry, change its direction and share knowledge?

The Road Ahead

As noted in Figure 16.2, the new top leader archetype is much different from years past. In today's market, top leaders will need to pivot away from the old rigid and vertical model to one that is flat and integrated. Top leaders will now be required to wear many more hats (operationally speaking) than in years past. Thus, their knowledge portfolio will be greater.

The term 'top leader' is fast becoming synonymous with many subtitles, such as chief communicator, chief partnership officer, chief outcomes officer, chief crisis negotiator, chief efficiency officer, chief visionary, chief strategist, chief facilitator, master change agent, chief knowledge officer and the like. Obviously, top leaders will have to rely on teams and other talent to be successful with all these endeavors. But, the key takeaway is that the new leader archetype will require a much more diverse skill set that leads to transformational outcomes. The basis for success will be rooted in managing change, thinking ahead, managing internal and external relationships, achieving transformational outcomes that are significant and sharing knowledge.

Summary

The only constant in today's world is change. The market has, is and continues to change—thus, so must the way organizations cultivate their leaders. The reality is that incremental change has been replaced with rapid, cyclical and disruptive evolutions. From a leadership perspective, the old way of measuring leadership potential via experience, credentials and political savvy is outdated and no longer effective.

The path forward for top leaders is simple: stay the traditional course and exit stage right or evolve and ride the wave to the new operational promised land. Successful top leaders will have to become aggressive change agents who possess the gifting to manage relationships in a way that results in significant outcomes. Simply put, outcomes are and will continue to be king, but not everyone will find the formula to break the code.

In closing, leadership is not always as easy as it seems. It's also a craft that is becoming increasingly difficult to navigate as the market continues to evolve. Leadership at its core is a worthy endeavor that provides those daring enough to take the ride with immeasurable intrinsic satisfaction, opportunities to help others and opportunities to learn from incredibly gifted colleagues.

Unfortunately, leadership archetypes of the past are fast becoming dated and struggle to work in today's disruptive market. If top leaders stick to the old playbook, they will struggle to be successful in the long term. Simply put, the old is out, and the new is in. The million-dollar question top leaders must answer is which category they fit in.

References

1. Forbes. *What Is Leadership?* 2013. www.forbes.com/sites/kevinkruse/2013/04/09/what-is-leadership/?sh=c850ed65b90c
2. American College of Healthcare Executives. *Hospital CEO Turnover at 18% for Fifth Year in a Row.* www.ache.org/about-ache/news-and-awards/news-releases/hospital-ceo-turnover

Chapter 17

Leveraging Maturity Models as Operational Truth Serum

Introduction

What does it really mean to mature? Maturity can be defined as, 'A measurement of the ability of an organization for continuous improvement in a particular discipline' (1). In layman's terms, many leaders refer to organizational or program maturity when operations are fully developed and consistently producing the desired outcomes. Unfortunately, many organizations struggle with achieving program or operational maturity. The real question is why?

In various thought leadership circles, common questions are often debated. Does organizational maturity really matter? Do mature programs or organizations outperform their less mature counterparts? How will leaders know when their operations are mature or at minimum moving in the right direction? Does all operational improvement equate to overall program or organizational maturity? Are programs maturing just because they have been doing 'something' a long time? These and other questions are answered in the following commentary.

Recently, a few thought leaders in the healthcare industry were debating their organization's progress related to the value equation. The value equation for most service industry organizations essentially starts with service, cost and quality. The conversation started with a revelatory statement by one of the leaders. The leader claimed, 'Our quality management system should be mature by now as we implemented it many years ago.'

DOI: 10.4324/9781003335108-18

The group was taken aback by the comment and began to challenge the remarks. The discussion produced interesting results. Subsequently, the group agreed that more data and discussion were needed to verify this and other assertions. As a result, a thought leader conducted a simple pilot study and later created a maturity model to track and validate the assertions. Let's take a closer look.

The Case Study

The team's pilot study focused on five major business units. All business units significantly contributed to the organization's service, cost and quality metrics. Each business unit implemented a quality management system at the same time years before the pilot study, was located in the same geographic region and impacted many tens of thousands of customers annually. There were also some anomalies and differences related to number of employees, leadership training related to performance improvement and operational outcomes.

The initial deep dive focused on five main attributes: quality management system structure, value outcomes or quality scores goal attainment, continuous improvement, strategic planning and standard work. The business units were ranked for each attribute as either above or below average as compared to this cohort for the enterprise. Regarding quality management system, each business unit was rated based on the structure of the system. Was it aligned with industry best practices and composed of the ideal components (inputs, process, outputs, governance and oversight), and did it produce the ideal outcomes tied to the value equation? Higher performers were rated as above average and their counterparts as below average.

For continuous improvement, each business unit was ranked high or low based on whether each had credentialed training in an improvement methodology, deployed resources to address opportunities and achieved measurable improvements. Another consideration was given if the business unit had a formally trained Six Sigma Black Belt leader. Those top performers achieved the basics plus published successful outcomes in industry best practice venues. This essentially contributed to external knowledge transfer. Again, the higher performers were rated as above average and their counterparts as below average.

Strategic planning was also considered as it's a crucial function to ensure both quality management system and continuous improvement are successful. The business units were rated as to if each had an annual planning process for gaps, goals, playbooks and budgets. Also, consideration was given if the process was conducted as planned and produced the desired outcomes as indicated in the strategic plan. Higher performers had a fine-tuned annual process with expected outcomes, whereas lower performers did not.

Standard work relates to documented organizational knowledge. Did each business unit have documented policies or work instructions to guide leaders and staff in completing work the same way each time? Were these documents housed in a knowledge management system and standardized? Were the documents audited frequently to ensure they maintained the required elements for standardization? The whole focus was to ensure the knowledge was captured, standardized, audited and readily available to end users.

Finally, the pilot scored each business unit on outcomes tied to service, cost and quality. At the end of the day, value is the desired end. Each customer expects high-quality services at reasonable prices. Each business unit was scored above or below average as compared to their counterparts in this cohort. Those higher performers produced better outcomes as compared to their counterparts. See Figure 17 for details.

	Unit 1	Unit 2	Unit 3	Unit 4	Unit 5
Quality Management System	Low	High	High	Low	Low
Continuous Improvement	High	High	High	Low	Low
Strategic Planning	Low	High	High	Low	Low
Standard Work	High	High	High	High	High
Value Scores (Quality, Service & Costs)	Low	High^	High^	Low	Low
Attributes Above Average	40%	100%*	80%*	20%	20%

Figure 17 Business Unit Analysis.

High = Above Average (Unit Comparison)
Low = Below Average (Unit Comparison)
* = Top Performer
^ = Statistically Significant at 95% Confidence Level or Greater

Once the pilot study parameters were established and initial data gathered, the team performed a simple analysis for gaps, commonalities and validations or lack thereof for quality management system maturity. The results were surprising. Two of the five business units were above average for all attributes, while 60% of the units scored less than average. Those top performers had quality management systems integrated with high-performing strategic planning and continuous improvement functions. Thus, they produced statistically significant outcomes related to service, cost and quality.

In contrast, most of the lower performing business units had a quality management system in place that met the basic requirements, but strategic planning and continuous improvement were not structured properly or integrated into the quality management system. Thus, value outcomes lagged and underperformed compared to the cohort. The top two business units also had Six Sigma Black Belt trained leaders, while their counterparts did not.

The takeaway is that perception was not reality. The leaders learned that even though all business units had a quality management system in place, they did not perform or mature at the same rate. Moreover, there are several compounding factors such as continuous improvement and strategic planning that greatly impact value outcomes for customers. What does this mean for maturity? Simply put, to mature organizations and programs, leaders should consider a basic framework to track progress or lack thereof over time.

The Framework

A maturity framework is much simpler than it sounds. Moreover, it is composed of basic business functions that leaders may assume are being considered or often take for granted. The key is not to overlook or undervalue the basics. A simple framework consists of three basic components: industry best practices for the respective program, measurement and a maturity model. See Figure 17.1 for details.

The starting point is industry best practices. Leaders should research what competitors, peers and top tier organizations in their field are doing and ensure their programs incorporate these best practices. We hear it said frequently, 'Why are we doing this?' The simplest answer should be that it's an industry best practice. It's also been said that ignorance is bliss. In today's market, if programs or organizations have their aim off target, they are

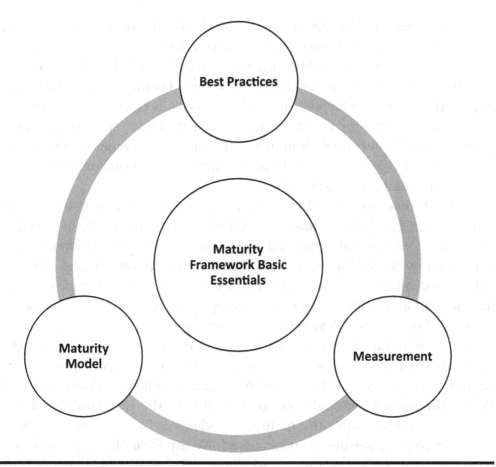

Figure 17.1 Maturity Framework Basic Essentials.

simply gifting their competitors a market advantage and placing their enterprise in a vulnerable position.

The second component of a maturity framework is measurement. Simply put, leaders don't know what they don't measure. As we learned in the case study, perception is not always reality. The key to measurement is to measure the right attributes, measure frequently and ensure what is being measured is visually displayed properly so stakeholders can see the forest and the trees. A good focal point would be key performance indicators tied to value. Most organizations begin with service, cost and quality metrics.

Finally, leaders should consider a maturity model. These models vary based on industry, scope and size of organizations. But, the key is simplicity. Organizations need a simple model that will display over time if the programs are maturing, stagnant or regressing. Let's take a closer look at a simple model.

After the leaders completed the case study for the five business units, the team created a simple maturity model piloted first in an essential program focused on service and quality. Once proven successful, the plan was to seed this model across the enterprise in various business units. The program impacted the entire enterprise and many thousands of customers annually. The maturity model focused on over a dozen attributes, such as strategic planning, top leadership commitment, measurable outcomes tied to safety and quality, standard work, performance improvement outcomes related to waste elimination and many others.

Each attribute was rated from 1 to 4 on a 4-point scale. Number 1 represented basic, 2 defining, 3 mature and 4 advanced. The attributes had three categories: foundational, structural and advanced. The foundational components were weighted higher as to their importance to quality and safety. The structural components were weighted next highest as they complemented the foundation. Finally, the advanced components were given the least amount of weight. See Figure 17.2 for an example.

Once the parameters were set, the team tracked the scores for each attribute monthly over several years and created a composite maturity score for the program. The program's maturity can be seen in Figure 17.3. Before the maturity model was created, 80% of the program's attributes were at best basic. After the maturity model was implemented, tracked and socialized, a seismic shift occurred. Nearly 90% of the program's attributes were either mature or advanced. The results pre- versus post-implementation of the model were significant at the 99% confidence level.

Attribute	Month 1	Weight
Strategic Planning*	1	20%
Program Structure*	2	20%
Performance Improvement**	2	15%
Standard Work*	3	20%
Top Leadership Commitment**	2	15%
Knowledge Transfer***	1	10%
Total Maturity Score	1.9	

* = Foundational (20% Weight)
** = Structural (15% Weight)
*** = Advanced (10% Weight)

Figure 17.2   Maturity Model

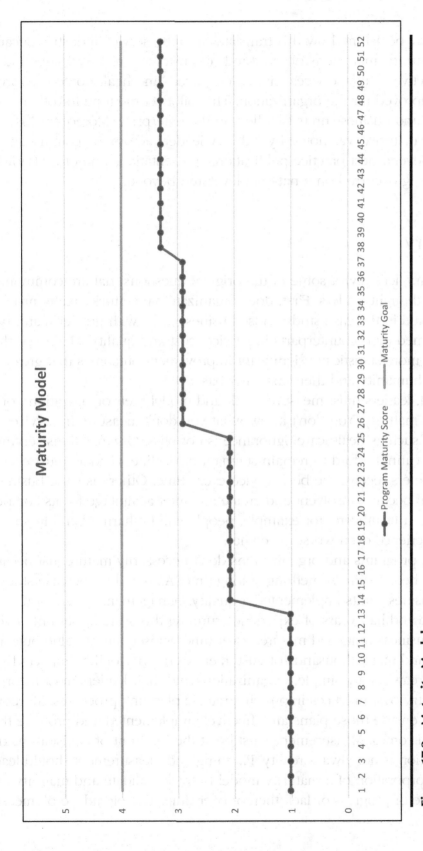

Figure 17.3 Maturity Model.

You may be asking how this translates into the service industry. Because of this maturity, many tens of thousands of customers received safer and more effective health services. Lives were saved, and health outcomes were greatly improved for the organization. This pilot set the tone for other programs and business units to follow in the enterprise. Moreover, this program's maturity was noted by industry leaders across the country and beyond. Several best practice publications, presentations and other knowledge sharing occurred on a national level and beyond.

Summary

In summary, let's revisit some of the original questions that are commonly posed by thought leaders. First, does organizational maturity really matter? As noted in the case study, those business units with greater maturity outperformed their counterparts in service, cost and quality. Moreover, they produced more statistically significant improvement outcomes that greatly impacted humanity and their customer base.

Second, leaders must measure, track and model their organization's or program's maturity. You don't know what you don't measure. In service industries such as healthcare, ignorance is not bliss. Organizations serving humanity cannot afford to remain stagnant or decline. Leaders must ensure that customers receive the best service every time. Otherwise, the business model will become insolvent and create a market advantage for its competitors. Also, in healthcare, for example, people will be harmed and in some cases experience even worse outcomes.

Finally, programs and organizations don't necessarily mature just because they have been doing 'something' a long time. As noted in the case study, all five business units implemented a quality management system at the same time and had years of experience running this system, but only two of the five business units had matured over time. Subsequently, value outcomes suffered, and many thousands of customers were unfavorably impacted.

The takeaways are simple. Organizations and their leaders must incorporate industry best practices into their strategic planning processes. Moreover, they must ensure those plans are effectively implemented and produce the desired outcomes. Measurement must be at the forefront of decision-making as perception is not always reality. Planning and measurement should lead to the incorporation of a maturity model to track, validate and magnify the importance of progress or lack thereof over time. The old adage of 'measure twice and cut once' can't be overstated. Leaders must plan, measure and validate their organization's or program's maturity to ensure they are exceeding customer requirements every time.

Reference

1. Wikipedia. Maturity model. 2021. https://en.wikipedia.org/wiki/Maturity_model

Conclusion

Leadership is a risky business. Leaders simply don't know what they don't measure. Change is the new norm, only constant and increasing over time. As change grows, so will risk and its effects on leaders, businesses and humanity. The key is that ignorance is never bliss.

As we learned, leadership is a perpetual fight along the journey. There will be amazing highs and earth-shaking lows. But, those that are fit for the fight and leverage risk to their advantage will land the knockout punch each time.

The leadership fight is really a series of perpetual decisions. Leaders will have to wrestle with decisions about taking or passing on next-level roles, who to promote, participating in activities that can enhance or destroy their brand, sharing information or holding it close to the vest, addressing variation and inconsistent performance outcomes, preventing and identifying burnout for themselves and others, investing in credentials or using time more wisely and so many other attributes of leadership. The key is that each decision and tollgate along the career journey is laden with risk. The only question is how many leaders will be fit enough for the fight?

Effective leaders are those who can identify, measure, assess and leverage risk to their advantage. The end goal is to minimize risk and maximize value. Leadership value takes many forms. Most importantly, leaders add value by enhancing service, quality, cost and efficiency.

Being fit for the fight simply helps leaders win big in high-risk environments.

DOI: 10.4324/9781003335108-19

Index

Note: Page numbers in *italics* indicate a figure on the corresponding page.

Printed in the United States
by Baker & Taylor Publisher Services

Printed in the United States
by Baker & Taylor Publisher Services